EIGHTY-EIGHT EASY-TO-MAKE AIDS
FOR OLDER PEOPLE
AND FOR SPECIAL NEEDS

EIGHTY-EIGHT EASY-TO-MAKE AIDS FOR OLDER PEOPLE

AND FOR SPECIAL NEEDS

by

Don Caston

HARTLEY & MARKS, PUBLISHERS

Published in the U.S.A. by
Hartley & Marks, Inc.
P. O. Box 147
Point Roberts, WA   98281

Published in Canada by
Hartley & Marks, Ltd.
3663 West Broadway
Vancouver, B.C.   V6R 2B8

Printed in the U.S.A.

First published in 1985 by Souvenir Press Ltd., London,
as *Easy to Make Aids For Elderly People* by Don Caston.

ISBN 0-88179-019-2 (paperback)

Library of Congress Cataloging-In-Publication Data

Caston, Don
[Easy to make aids for elderly people]
Eighty-eight easy-to-make aids for older people / Don Caston.
p.   cm.
Previously published as: Easy to make aids for elderly people.
1985.
ISBN 0-88179-019-2 (alk. paper : pbk.) : $11.95
1. Woodwork. 2. Self-help devices for the disabled--Design and construction. 3. Aged--Home care--Equipment and supplies.
I. Title.
TT200.C38   1988
684.1--dc19   88-25797

Typeset by The Typeworks

To Senor Francisco Palmer y Senora Amparo Benito, y
Senor José Martin Gonzales y Senora Andrea Gail Santos y
Hij Calixto Martin Gail y Yolanda Martin Gail
who have made me so welcome in their Spain.

CONTENTS

INTRODUCTION

As I grow older I am beginning to feel the need for a "little-something-or-other" to help me do a number of jobs that not so long ago I did without thinking. Perhaps anatomically I am changing, with my arms getting shorter and my legs longer, because I now seem to have a problem reaching down to put on my shoes, and an even greater one when I want to take them off. I am also beginning to find that things about my home are changing; for instance, shelves are getting higher, the bottom drawer of the chest of drawers in my bedroom is now much lower than it used to be, and it has also become much heavier and more difficult to open and close. The more I think about it, there does not seem to be one room that has not changed in some way or other. Out in the garden it's the same story—all the tools are heavier and definitely harder to use, and when it comes to weeding, the weeds now grow at an alarming rate with roots intent on going down to Australia.

The last thing I want is to be surrounded by gadgets, but if they allow me to keep my independence I shall accept them as part of growing older. You will note that I did not use the word old because that is something I shall never accept.

I think the same thoughts will go through my mind if one day it is suggested that I should have a wheelchair or some other hospital-type pieces of furniture in the home. Before I accept these chrome-plated and plastic things I shall want to know if my favorite armchair, dining room chair, or whatever it is they suggest should be changed, cannot be safely modified so that I can continue to live with all the goods and chattels which have been part of my life for so long. There is no way that my home is even going to start looking like a hospital ward.

It was with all this in mind that I was prompted to write this book. I hope to show that it is possible to have a little help around the home which will not advertize the fact that you are getting older, or that you are a handicapped person.

It is not suggested that you yourself should make all the things your medical adviser considers would help you, but there is no reason why you should not lend a hand when family and friends are making them for you. Alternatively, having taught in schools, I know that there are many teachers of technical workshops who are looking for projects like these which involve a little design, making something useful, and, possibly even more important, working with the community; they may be willing to get their pupils to make small items for you.

Some of the aids are, of course, available through suppliers of appliances, but the advantage of having them made for you is that, with the help of your medical adviser, they will be tailored to your own exact requirements—there will be no need to push cushions or pillows between you and the chair to make you comfortable, the foot rest will be at exactly the right height, and lights will be in the best places for you personally.

It is very important that you seek medical advice before making or having made any of the aids suggested in this book. Your medical adviser will be very pleased to help you, and will very often make some good suggestions from a medical point of view. Your adviser will also be able to teach you how to use the aids.

Note: If you need help with making alterations or installations, ask your neighborhood community services or senior service organizations.

EIGHTY-EIGHT EASY-TO-MAKE AIDS FOR OLDER PEOPLE

AND FOR SPECIAL NEEDS

Symbols For Materials Used in the Book

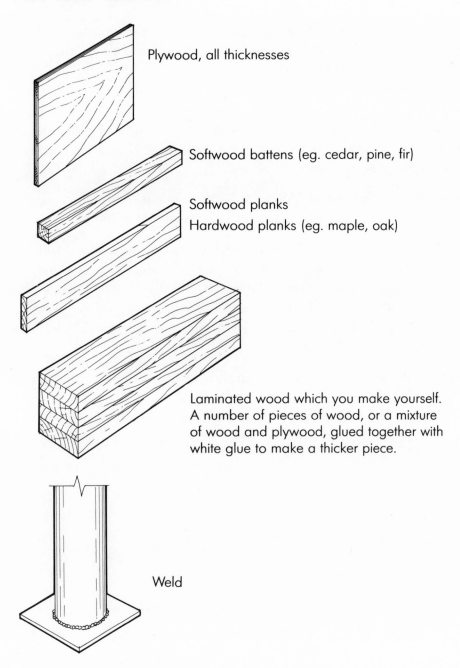

Plywood, all thicknesses

Softwood battens (eg. cedar, pine, fir)

Softwood planks
Hardwood planks (eg. maple, oak)

Laminated wood which you make yourself. A number of pieces of wood, or a mixture of wood and plywood, glued together with white glue to make a thicker piece.

Weld

Glossary of Construction Terms

Fix: Throughout this book "fix" means to join together by glue and nails, glue and screws, nuts and bolts, or self-tapping screws. In the case of dowelling, it means to glue into a drilled hole.

Cut Out: Cut out means sawing wood with any kind of saw.

Pilot Holes: These are holes drilled through the wood before driving home a nail or screw, to minimize the risk of splitting it. The diameter of the hole is usually about half that of the nail or screw.

Drive Fit: A drive fit is when a dowel has to be knocked into the hole with a hammer. A little glue is put in the hole first. Care must be taken not to split the wood.

Marking Out: This means drawing lines and making marks on the wood with a pencil to indicate where to saw, drill a hole, or shape it in some way. If a line is drawn in the wrong place, draw a wavy line through it, because it is all too easy to saw down the wrong line. When all the marking out has been completed, spend a few moments checking the lines to make sure that they are dimensionally in the right place.

Laminating: It is not always possible to buy a short length of wood or a piece of plywood in the width or thickness required for a particular job. This problem can often be overcome by glueing pieces of wood together as illustrated. Apply the glue evenly but not thickly, and keep the wood under pressure while the glue dries.

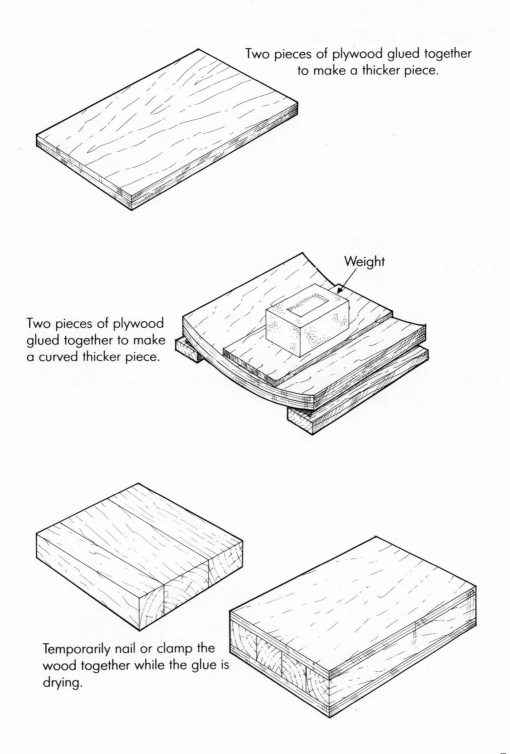

Two pieces of plywood glued together to make a thicker piece.

Weight

Two pieces of plywood glued together to make a curved thicker piece.

Temporarily nail or clamp the wood together while the glue is drying.

Safety

A habit must be formed of regularly checking the home and listing all the items which are starting to need attention. **Don't wait until there is an accident.**

As soon as a light starts to flicker when the switch is touched, an electrical wire starts to fray, or there is the slightest smell of gas, a loose screw, a water leak—whatever it is, get it seen to **at once.**

Home and furniture modifications must also be examined carefully and regularly; not only for the workmanship, but because you may have changed a little, making another alteration necessary. Never put your independence at stake.

Read all the booklets you can on home safety.

Using Non-Toxic Materials

Because certain modern materials introduce chemical pollutants into the home, it is recommended that anyone constructing the aids in this book follow these guidelines:

- Always use *exterior* grade plywood. It contains less formaldehyde than interior grades.

- Always seal plywood thoroughly with *2 coats* of lacquer-based varnish or urethane varnish. Take special care to seal all edges. This considerably reduces outgassing of formaldehyde.

- When painting plywood, always use a latex sealer coat *first*, and then your choice of finish coat.

- *Avoid* exterior paint for indoor use, as it is most permeable to formaldehyde. Marine paint is very durable, and the best choice for a final coat of paint if durability is a priority.

- *Avoid* plastic glue or special chemical glues.

- *Plain white glue* is very safe, and if glued pieces are clamped securely for 12 hours, no other glue will be needed.

For detailed information about the safety of other home building materials, see *Your Home, Your Health, and Well-Being,* by D. Rousseau. Hartley & Marks, Publishers. 1988.

Buying the Wood

To make modifications to some furniture less noticeable, the wood may have to be stained instead of painted. To get a truer match, it is often better to use second-hand wood of the same type. This can be obtained by buying a piece of old furniture and carefully taking it apart. Make sure the wood is sound and completely free from rot before purchase.

For any other wood required, it is best to go to the local lumber yard. Here will be found a good selection of both lumber and plywood. The cheapest way to buy wood is from places which sell off-cuts. With a tape measure, check each piece you pick out to make sure it is large enough and of the right thickness. Always check for faults such as end splits, knots, twisting and bowing, and de-laminating of the layers of the plywood.

Also make sure that any plywood is not too flexible. A larger piece usually bends more easily in one direction than the other, so if a strip of plywood, cut lengthwise, for instance, is not stiff enough, try to find a piece that has been cut crosswise or from another part of the sheet.

Throughout this book the thickness of plywood is given in both inches and metric sizes.

Tool Kit

It is not necessary to go out and spend a small fortune on a boxful of tools before work can start. Practically all the furniture modifications and aids can be made with only eight hand tools. As there are no such things as good cheap tools, it is advisable to buy the best you can afford: tools made by a well-known company will last a lifetime, and if used and stored properly will not need to be sharpened too often. Always keep tools well out of a child's reach.

The tools required are:
Crosscut handsaw (6 to 12 points per inch)
Backsaw, 10″ (25 cm)
Coping saw
Hacksaw
Claw hammer, approximately 8 oz
Robertson screwdriver (4 sizes; square heads)
Hand drill and a set of twist drills
Plane, preferably with replaceable blades if you are not good at sharpening on a stone
Tape measure, 6 feet (2 meters), with both inches and metric units

How to Use Your Tools

Sawing

The *handsaw* is used for cutting large pieces of wood such as sheets of plywood, wooden planks, and sections.

The *backsaw* should only be used for cutting small pieces of wood such as battens and narrow pieces of plywood.

Both of these saws make a cut that is smooth enough to be finished with sandpaper. Do not hold these saws too tightly, or have the forefinger pointing down

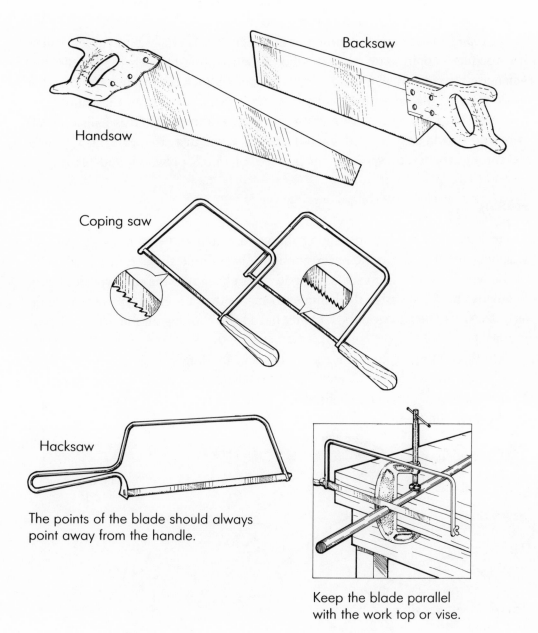

Backsaw

Handsaw

Coping saw

Hacksaw

The points of the blade should always
point away from the handle.

Keep the blade parallel
with the work top or vise.

9

the blade like a child pretending his hand is a gun. Use the handsaw at an angle of about 45°, but when using the backsaw start the cut at a slight angle, then slowly flatten it and saw straight across the wood.

The *coping saw* is used for cutting out such shapes as circles and curves. When it is used as a coping saw the teeth should be pointing towards the handle, but when used to cut a small piece of wood on a bench hook (instructions below), the blade must be turned around so that the teeth point away from the handle.

The *hacksaw* is intended for cutting thin pieces of metal, such as nails or thick wire, and should only be used when the metal is held in a vise. It can also be used for cutting wooden dowels and small pieces of wood, plywood, and plastic.

Nailing

As no big nails are used in making the various items in this book, a hammer weighing about 8 oz is quite heavy enough. Always hold the hammer by the end of the handle and learn to strike the nail squarely so that the nail will not bend. Regularly check the face of the hammer to ensure that it is clean and very smooth, as this will also help to stop the hammer head from slipping off the nail and bending it.

Grip the nail firmly between the thumb and forefinger.

Note: Nails come in two types, headed (eg. common nails and shingle nails) and headless (eg. finishing nails).

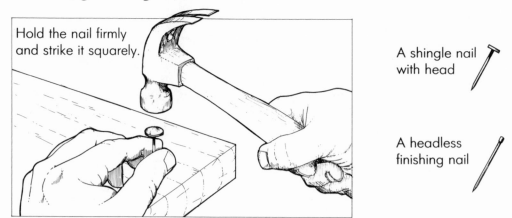

Hold the nail firmly and strike it squarely.

A shingle nail with head

A headless finishing nail

Screwing

Screwdrivers come in many shapes and sizes, and it is important to pick the one which fits the screw slot properly. If it does not, there is a good chance of the slot being damaged and left dangerously sharp. It is therefore a good idea to buy a set of screwdrivers which will cover most screw sizes. However, these problems can be avoided by using Robertson screws and screwdrivers (square ends, 4 sizes). Another way of damaging the slot, so that it becomes dangerous, is to fail to keep the screwdriver upright. When this happens, it is not unusual for a thin and very sharp sliver of metal to be left sticking up.

Always counter-bore when using countersunk screws, so that the head is always flush with or slightly below the surface. There is no need to do this if brass cups are used. (Refer to Glue and Screw Construction, under METHODS OF CONSTRUCTION, below.)

Drilling

When using a hand drill or twist drill, do not apply too much pressure; let the drill do the cutting. The most important thing to learn is to keep the drill at 90° to the job. A twist drill is used to make a hole exactly the size and depth required. A special masonry drill will be necessary if holes have to be made in brick walls and concrete. It is advisable to employ an expert for drilling some materials, such as glass and ceramic tiles.

When fixing something to a solid wall, it is best to buy specially made plugs which are tapped into a drilled hole so that, in effect, it is like driving a screw into a piece of wood. Advice on which type to use can be obtained from the local hardware store.

A countersink bit is used to open up a hole so that the head of the screw is level with the surface or very slightly below it.

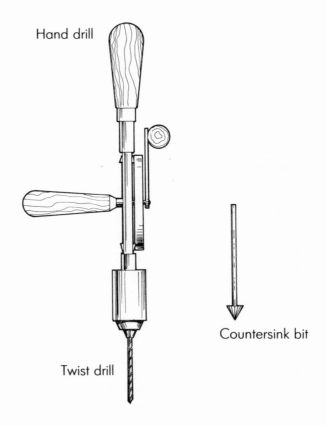

Hand drill

Countersink bit

Twist drill

Planing

The types of saw listed in the tool kit have been chosen because they do not leave the wood too rough, and a sandpaper finish is possible; but sometimes cheap off-cuts will need planing. As this is where you will save money, it is a good idea to learn how to use a plane.

One-handed planing is possible after a little practice. The wood is held upright and pressed against the sandpaper board batten as shown in the drawing. If you have a vise to hold the wood, then both hands should be used to grip the plane. At the start of the cut, apply a little extra pressure to the front handle, then even pressure with both hands until just before you reach the end of the wood, when a little extra pressure is applied to the back of the plane.

Always make sure that you plane with the grain of the wood and keep the blade sharp.

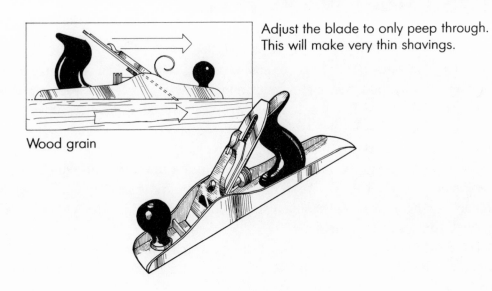

Adjust the blade to only peep through. This will make very thin shavings.

Wood grain

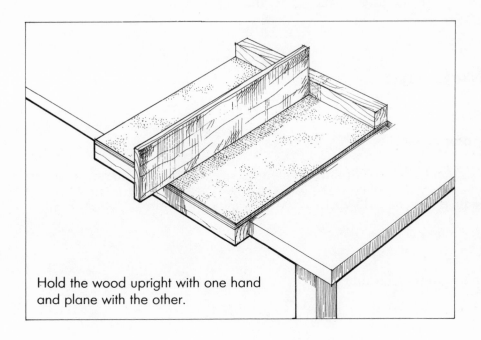

Hold the wood upright with one hand and plane with the other.

If You Have No Workshop

If you have no workshop, garage, or spare room to work in, your kitchen can be temporarily converted into one. A quick and easy way to solve the problem is to make the work top the first job. It not only protects the table and gives a firm base to work on, but it makes the job of clearing up and putting everything away quick and simple. The work top makes kitchen table carpentry possible.

The second job is to make a kitchen chair into a saw horse on which to cut larger pieces of wood. The seat top gives protection to the seat of the chair while you are sawing. If possible, choose a strong chair and one low enough for you to rest your knee on comfortably.

The third item to make is the bench hook, which will provide a firm base on which to saw small bits of wood. This piece of equipment can be used on the work top.

Finally, make a few sandpaper boards for various grades of paper and some sandpaper blocks in a range of sizes and shapes.

Now, with the tools, some white glue, nails, and screws, your workshop is ready for action.

Work Top

Shopping List

A. Base: plywood ⅜″ (8 mm), minimum size 12″ × 20″ (30 cm × 50 cm)

B. Batten: softwood 1″ × 1″ × 20″ (25 mm × 25 mm × 50 cm)

C. One thin cork tile

Construction: Glue and Nail

Instructions

1. Fix batten B to base A.
2. Cut cork tile into 1″ (25 mm) strips, and glue to underside of the base and inside edge of the batten.

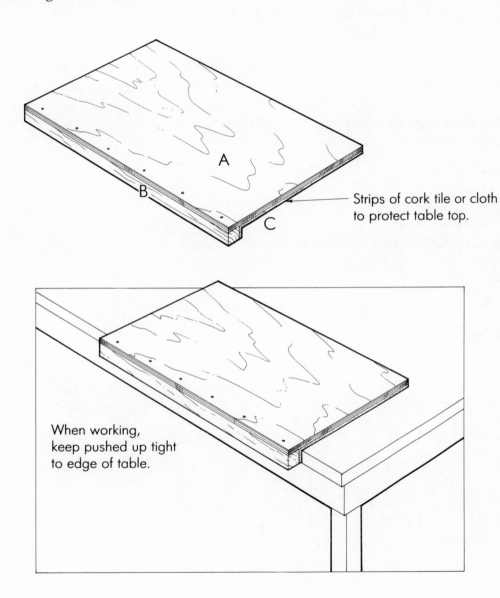

Strips of cork tile or cloth to protect table top.

When working, keep pushed up tight to edge of table.

Seat Top

Shopping List

A. Seat cover: plywood ⅜" (8 mm) × width of chair seat plus 2" (5 cm) × depth of chair plus 1" (25 mm)

B. Battens, 3 required: softwood 1" × 1" (25 mm × 25 mm) × length to suit chair seat size

Construction: Glue and Nail

Instructions

1. Fix battens B to the three sides of the seat cover A so that it makes an easy fit over the chair seat.
2. Glue cloth to the underside to give added protection to the chair seat.

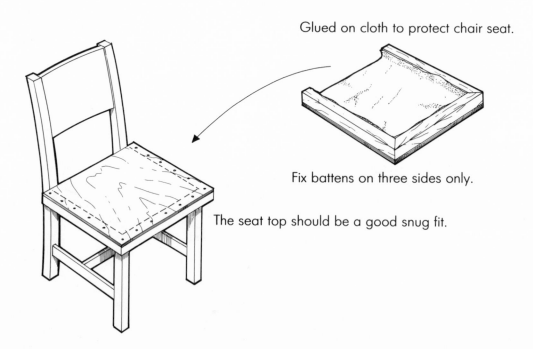

Glued on cloth to protect chair seat.

Fix battens on three sides only.

The seat top should be a good snug fit.

Bench Hook

Shopping List

A. Base: plywood ⅜″ × 7″ × 12″ (8 mm × 18 cm × 30 cm)

B. Wood rest: softwood 1½″ × 1½″ × 5″ (4 cm × 4 cm × 13 cm)

C. Edge: softwood 1″ × 1″ × 7″ (25 mm × 25 mm × 18 cm)

Construction: Glue and Nail

Instructions

1. Fix wood rest B to base A as shown on drawing.
2. Fix edge C to underside of base A.

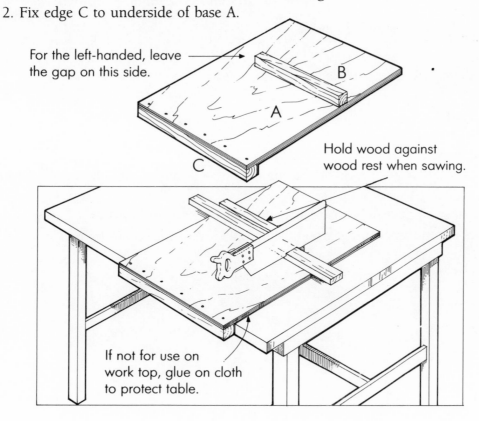

For the left-handed, leave the gap on this side.

Hold wood against wood rest when sawing.

If not for use on work top, glue on cloth to protect table.

Sandpaper Boards and Sanding Blocks

For many smoothing jobs it is better to rub the wood on the sandpaper than the sandpaper on the wood. The finish of the piece of plywood or softwood will be smoother and more square when it has been rubbed on a sheet of sandpaper glued to a piece of plywood, because only the high spots will come into contact with the rough cutting surface of the paper. Buy only good quality sandpaper. To maintain a good cutting surface, keep it free of wood dust by regular brushing. Make several boards so that a range of grades of sandpaper is always ready for use.

Shopping List

A. Base: plywood ¼″ × 9″ × 12″ (6 mm × 23 cm × 30 cm)

B. Battens, 2 required: 1″ × 1″ × 12″ (25 mm × 25 mm × 30 cm)

C. Sandpaper: a range of grades

Construction: Glue and Nail

Instructions

1. Fix battens B to base A.
2. Glue sandpaper to each side, using only a very thin coat of glue.

Sandpaper blocks can be made in a wide range of shapes and sizes. Glue various grades of sandpaper to the wood, using only a very thin coat of glue.

The size of the board is determined by the size of the sandpaper available.

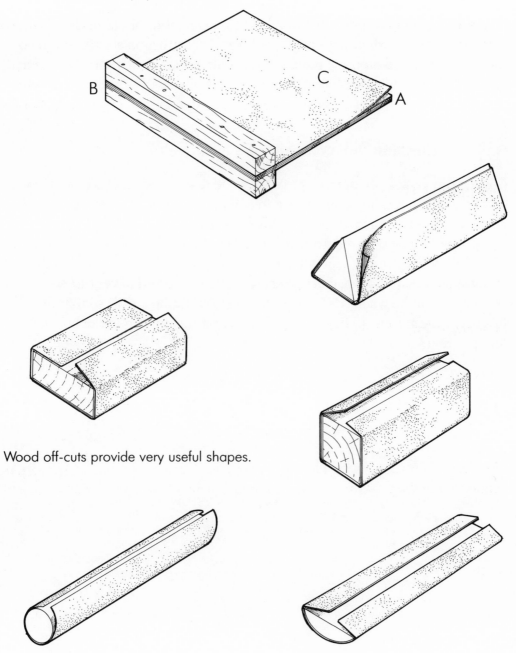

Wood off-cuts provide very useful shapes.

19

Methods of Construction

As it can safely be assumed that most people have used, or can learn to use, a hammer and a screwdriver, the three methods of construction chosen throughout this book are based on these fundamental skills: using glue and nails, glue and screws, and nuts and bolts. The latter method is not used very often.

Study the drawings of the first two methods carefully before you start work.

Glue and Finishing Nail Construction

Glueing and nailing two or more pieces of wood together gives a very strong joint, so long as the pieces to be joined are free of paint and oil, are smooth, flat, and touch one another throughout their whole length.

Use a white glue of a well-known brand; apply it evenly and not too thickly to both sides to be joined. Wipe off surplus glue before it has had time to dry.

Always fully support wood before using the hammer. And **never** leave any nails sticking out of the wood. Use a nail punch to set headless nails so that they are just below the surface. If they are knocked deeper the little holes can be filled before painting.

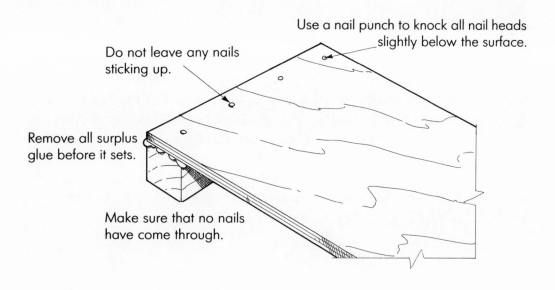

Use a nail punch to knock all nail heads slightly below the surface.

Do not leave any nails sticking up.

Remove all surplus glue before it sets.

Make sure that no nails have come through.

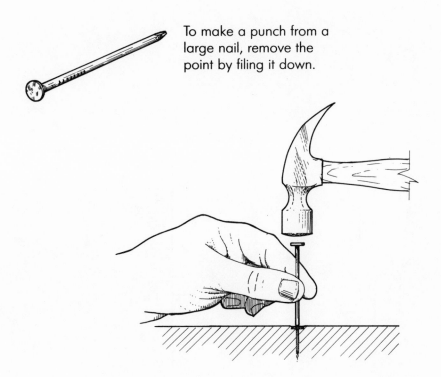

To make a punch from a large nail, remove the point by filing it down.

Rest the punch on the nail head and strike it squarely and firmly.

21

Glue and Screw Construction

As it is easy to remove screws, this method of construction is used when adjustments may have to be made at a later time. No glue is used for the trial assembly.
1. Drill a hole in one piece of wood A, which the screw will only just go through.
2. Countersink the hole so that the screw head will be slightly below the surface.
3. Drill a hole in the other piece of wood B, half the diameter of the first one, and half the depth of the screw length.
4. Screw the two pieces of wood together, but not so hard that the wood around the screw thread cracks. This would make the screw keep turning, and the joint insecure. For final assembly apply glue before screwing together.

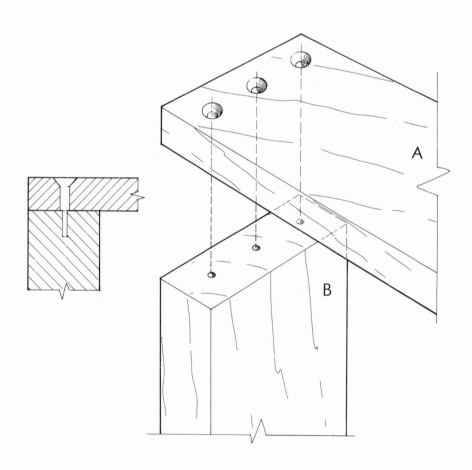

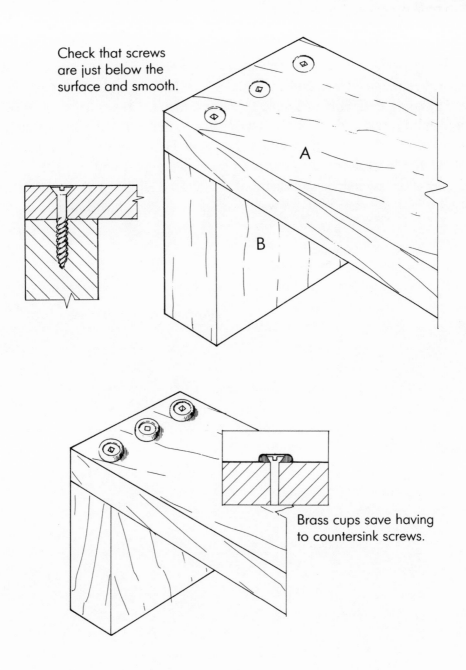

Check that screws
are just below the
surface and smooth.

A

B

Brass cups save having
to countersink screws.

23

Glues

Modern glues are so good that it is now much easier for the do-it-yourself enthusiast, as well as the kitchen table carpenter, to make things. Many jobs can be successfully completed without having to make difficult joints, such as mortise and tenon and dovetails. These not only take time to make, but if not accurately cut will not be very strong. In this book it is suggested that those who do not have the skills or the equipment should either glue and nail or glue and screw. Sometimes it is only necessary to glue and clamp. If the finished job has to be washed a lot or left outside, it is better to use a waterproof glue such as boat builders use.

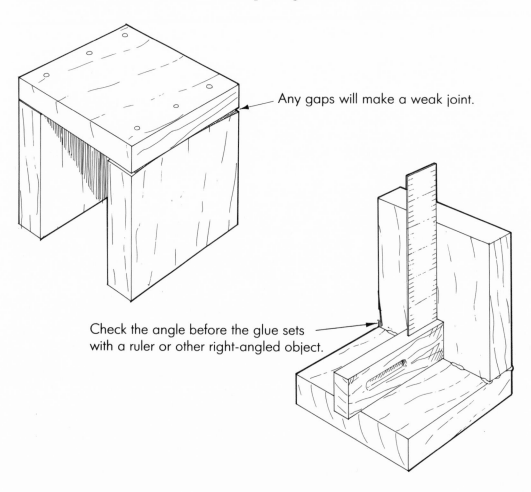

Any gaps will make a weak joint.

Check the angle before the glue sets
with a ruler or other right-angled object.

Painting

Most local paint suppliers carry a wide range of colors, and many even have special machines which will mix almost any shade required while you wait. It is important that all modifications to furniture and aids that you make or get made are painted or stained, so that they do not stand out too much from the rest of your home.

Besides choice of color, you will also have to decide which type of paint you buy—oil bound or water-based. The latter is by far the easier to use. No expensive solvents are needed and small changes in color can be made by adding a little watercolor paint, so you have no excuse for not having a very good match. However, where a large area is to be painted, or if the item is to be kept near you, be sure the paint you use does not have an unpleasant odor after it dries. While water-based paints dry more quickly than oil paints, many of them continue to emit an odor over a very long period of time. Most oil paints, on the other hand, stop emitting an odor once they have dried.

As with tools, there is no such thing as a good cheap paint brush, so buy the best you can afford. If you use water-based paint, the brushes can be washed under a running cold water tap.

Painting and finishing is done in four stages:

1. Fill all holes, surface blemishes, cracks, and corners that could become dirt traps, with a filler, plastic wood, or putty. Allow plenty of time to dry, if possible overnight. There are two basic types of filler to choose from: those bought in powder form, to which water is added to make a putty-like mixture, and those supplied ready mixed in cans or plastic tubes. It is a good idea to make filling and painting jobs the last task before packing up for the day, to give plenty of drying time.

2. Rub down the whole surface to be painted, including the removal of all sharp corners and edges, with sandpaper. Start with a coarse grade and finish with a fine one.

3. Apply two *thin* coats of paint, rubbing down with a fairly fine sandpaper between each coat.

4. Apply two *thin* top coats, again rubbing down between each coat.

Painting is not as difficult as most people think, and if the procedures just described are adhered to, the following three major problems will be eliminated.

- Runs, like little rivers down the wood, which will take a very long time to dry and are then difficult to remove.
- Drips on the floor.
- Long waits while the paint dries.

Always stir the paint well before starting to use it, unless it is of the non-drip variety. Dip the brush only ½" (1.5 cm) into the paint and wipe off any excess on the lip of the can.

Read the manufacturer's instructions and keep to them.

Staining

Much furniture is colored and polished so that the wood's grain can be seen. In order to match this finish a stain must be used. There is a wide range of both latex and oil stains on the market, but the easiest to use is probably the latex one. If the manufacturer's instructions are followed to the letter a good match can be obtained. Finish with a clear varnish.

THE KITCHEN

As so much time has to be spent in the kitchen, and much of it on your feet, changes should be made so that it becomes an easier place to work in. This may mean some fairly big alterations, but it will be well worth the short upheaval while they are being made. For example, shelves can be lowered, as can cabinets which are screwed to the wall.

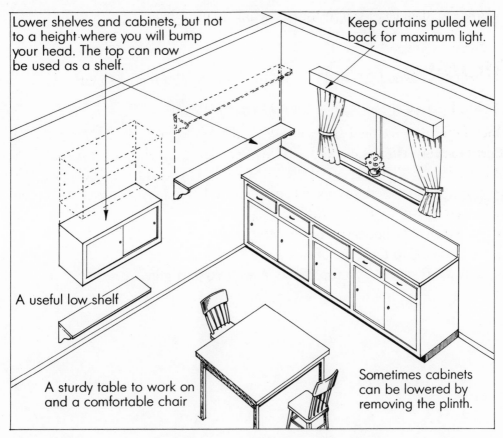

Lower shelves and cabinets, but not to a height where you will bump your head. The top can now be used as a shelf.

Keep curtains pulled well back for maximum light.

A useful low shelf

A sturdy table to work on and a comfortable chair

Sometimes cabinets can be lowered by removing the plinth.

Note: Sliding doors can be stiff to open. Take them off by lifting up and out.

Work Top

This very useful working surface will not move away from you while it is being used. As it is so light and has a good edge to grip, it can easily be carried to any room in the house and used on any table, even though it is mainly intended for kitchen use. It will not matter how dirty it gets, just take it to the sink for washing.

Shopping List

A. Tray: plywood ¼″ × 10″ × 18″ (6 mm × 25 cm × 45 cm)

B. Batten: softwood 1″ × 1″ × 18″ (25 mm × 25 mm × 45 cm)

C. Batten: softwood ½″ × 1″ × 18″ (12 mm × 25 mm × 45 cm)

D. Rigid plastic sheet: 9½″ × 18″ (24 cm × 45 cm)

Construction: Glue and Nail

Instructions

1. Fix batten B to underside of tray A.
2. Fix batten C to top edge of tray A.
3. Glue plastic sheet D to top of tray A with contact glue.

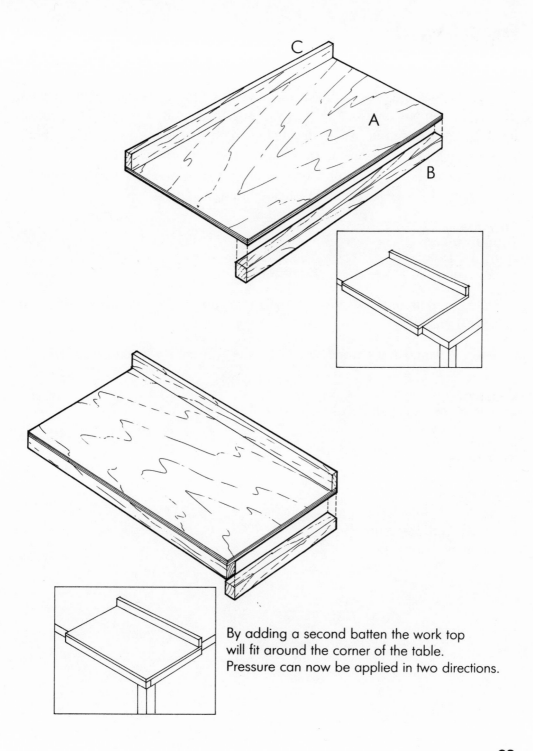

By adding a second batten the work top
will fit around the corner of the table.
Pressure can now be applied in two directions.

29

Foot Stool

Putting on shoes and socks, tying laces, and cutting toenails need not be such an effort if you can put your foot up on a little angled stool. It can be made to almost any height and it is up to you to decide how high after doing a few tests. If both feet are going to be put on the stool together, double the width. (Optional: To keep feet from sliding off, a soft fabric, doubled to about ½″ (12 mm), can be attached at the back edge, using self-stick fabric fastening.)

Shopping List

A. Top: softwood ¾″ × 5″ × 9″ (19 mm × 13 cm × 23 cm)

B. Sides, 2 required: softwood ¾″ × height to suit × 7½″ (19 mm × height to suit × 19 cm)

C. Ends, 2 required: softwood ¾″ × 2″ × 4″ (19 mm × 5 cm × 10 cm)

Construction: Glue and Nail

Instructions

1. Cut angles in sides B to suit.
2. Fix ends C to sides B.
3. Fix top A to assembly B.
3. Sandpaper and paint.

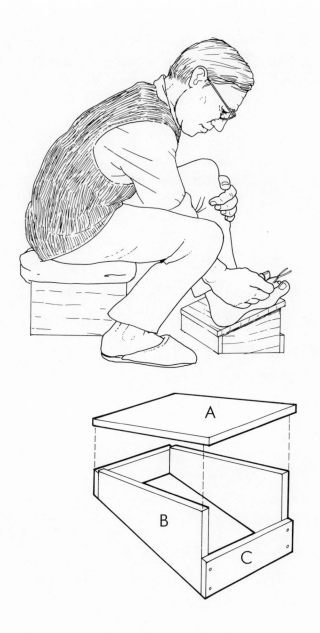

A

B

C

Wheeled Trolley

A wheeled trolley can be pushed to where it is needed. The sizes given are guide dimensions only and should be changed to make the trolley just right for you. You may find later that you need another one—one for the kitchen for dishes, knives, and other gadgets which you find you need for preparing food, the second in the living room to hold all the things for daily living, including hobbies and other pastimes.

Two methods of construction are suggested and both give good results. Wooden battens or angle brackets may be used.

Shopping List

A. Top: plywood ½″ × 10″ × 24″ (11 mm × 25 cm × 60 cm)

B. Sides, 2 required: plywood ½″ × 10″ × 24″ (11 mm × 25 cm × 60 cm)

C. Shelf: plywood ½″ × 8″ × 24″ (11 mm × 20 cm × 60 cm)

D. Base: plywood ½″ × 10″ × 24″ (11 mm × 25 cm × 60 cm)

E. Back: plywood ¼″ × 22½″ × 24″ (6 mm × 56 cm × 60 cm)

F. Shelf back small: plywood ½″ × 1½″ × 24″ (11 mm × 4 cm × 60 cm)

G. Shelf front, 3 required: plywood ½″ × 1½″ × 24″ (11 mm × 4 cm × 60 cm)

H. Cup hooks, 5 or 6 required

I. Softwood battens cut from ¾″ × ¾″ × 15 ft (20 mm × 20 mm × 4.5 m) *or* angle brackets, about 28 required

J. Screws for angle brackets, about 80 required

K. Casters, 4 required: wheel size about 2″ (5 cm) diameter

Construction: Wooden battens—glue and nail
                     Angle brackets—wood screws

Instructions

1. Fix battens or angle brackets to parts A, C, D, and E as illustrated.
2. Assemble as illustrated.
3. Sandpaper thoroughly.
4. Fix casters in the corners of base D.
5. Finish by painting or staining.

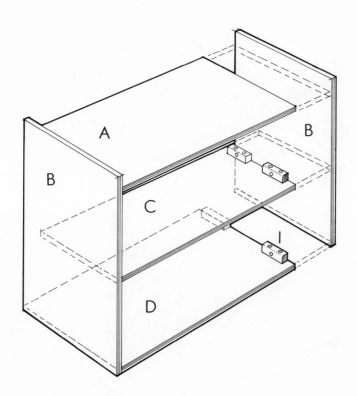

The basic construction can be seen when one of the sides B is taken off.

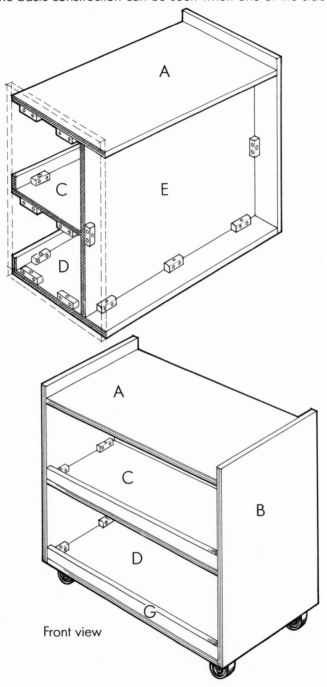

Front view

Plywood and batten construction

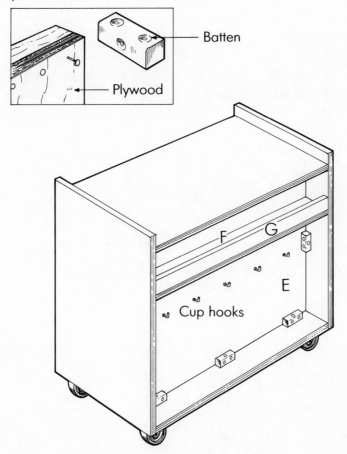

Batten

Plywood

F   G

E

Cup hooks

View of back showing hanging space

Plinth

The lower shelves and drawers of a number of pieces of furniture are often too low to be comfortably reached. The plinth is one item which should be made by a professional, who should also fix the furniture to it. If there is the slightest chance of it being unstable and falling on you when the doors or drawers are open, then it must be attached to the wall.

Never do any modifications to gas or electrical appliances yourself. The gas and electricity authorities have trained staff to help and advise you.

It is not possible to give any dimensions as these will depend on the size and the weight the plinth will have to carry.

A plinth raises the cabinet to be comfortably reached.

This plinth tends to collect dust.

This plinth will prevent dust collecting.

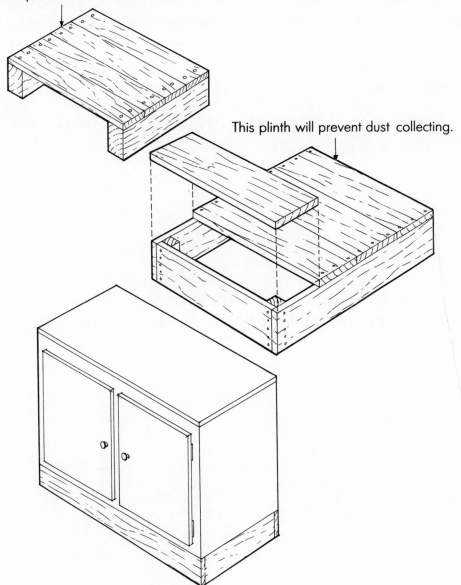

Plywood can be used for light cabinets.

Cutting Aid and Board

This is a useful little kitchen tool for cutting, slicing, and scraping. The size of the handle is important, so grip various pieces of dowel until one is found which feels comfortable when it is held tightly. Whatever handle size is finally decided upon, the nails should stick out about 2″ (5 cm).

Shopping List

A. Handle: wooden dowel, diameter and length to suit the hand

B. Galvanized nails, 9 required

C. Cutting board: hardwood about ⅝″ × 6″ × 6″ (14 mm × 15 cm × 15 cm)

Instructions

1. Mark out the positions for the nails.
2. Drill the nine holes to provide drive fits for the nails.
3. Hammer the nails through the handle A.
4. Finish by sandpapering the ends of the handle and the cutting board C.

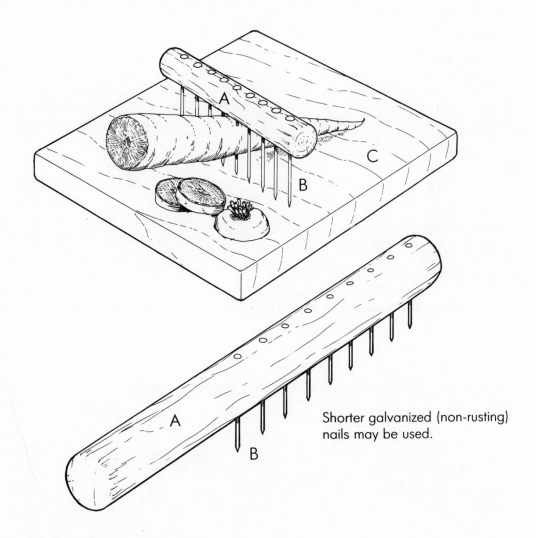

Shorter galvanized (non-rusting) nails may be used.

The size of the handle must suit the hand's grip.

Bread and Butter Spreader

If the butter is not too hard and the bread has not been cut too thin, the job of buttering a slice of bread is made much easier. (A butter spreader will be easier to use than a knife.)

Shopping List

A. Base board: softwood ¾″ × 6″ × 8″ (19 mm × 15 cm × 20 cm)

B. Table batten: softwood 1″ × 1″ × 6″ (25 mm × 25 mm × 15 cm)

C. Table batten: softwood 1″ × 1″ × 7″ (25 mm × 25 mm × 18 cm)

D. Bread rest battens, 2 required: ¼″ × ¼″ × 6″ (6 mm × 6 mm × 15 cm)

Construction: Glue and Nail

Instructions

1. Fix table batten B to base board A.
2. Fix table batten C to base board A.
3. Fix bread battens D to top of base board A.
4. Finish by sandpapering to remove all sharp corners and edges.
5. (Optional: Seal surface of A with a clear urethane varnish.)

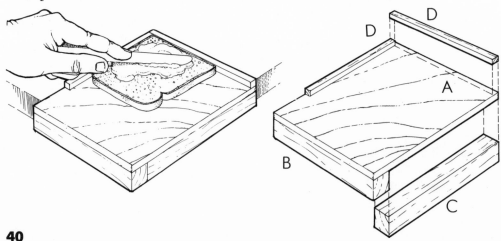

Cutting Board

This can be made in much the same way as the bread and butter spreader, except that it has spikes to hold the food. The position of the spikes can be changed if they do not hold the food firmly enough. Do not make the spikes too long—usually 1″ (25 mm) is enough. If nails are used, make sure that they are well dried after washing to prevent rusting, or better still, use galvanized (non-rusting) nails.

Shopping List

A. Base board: hardwood ¼″ × 8″ × 8″ (6 mm × 20 cm × 20 cm) or ¾″ × 8″ × 8″ (19 mm × 20 cm × 20 cm) softwood

B. Base batten: softwood 1″ × 1″ × 8″ (25 mm × 25 mm × 20 cm)

C. Base batten: softwood 1″ × 1″ × 7″ (25 mm × 25 mm × 18 cm)

D. Spikes, 9 required: nails about 1¼″ (3 cm) long, and heavy gauge

Construction: Glue and Nail

Instructions

1. Drill 9 holes as illustrated. These must be much smaller than the diameter of the spikes D.
2. Fix base batten B to base board A.
3. Fix base batten C to base board A.
4. Hammer the spikes D from the under side of the base board A.
5. Sandpaper to finish.

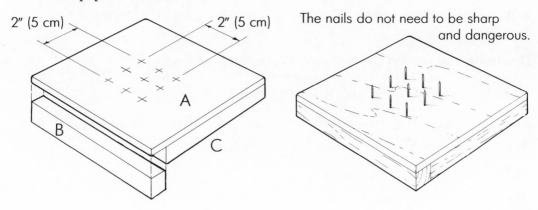

2″ (5 cm)   2″ (5 cm)   The nails do not need to be sharp and dangerous.

A   B   C

Kitchen Table Working Surface

A lot of time is spent in the kitchen preparing food, so it is very important to make sure that the kitchen table is made an easy place to work on. If this is done, preparing food will become much less tiring, and then there is no excuse for not being more adventurous with your diet, and cooking those dishes you used to enjoy so much. The working surface can be made any size or shape and can, should the table be too high, be made to fit underneath, as illustrated. In the interest of hygiene, the top and sides should have a hard plastic surface. Several variations can be made, as shown in the illustrations.

Shopping List for Work Surface (Example sizes.)

A. Board: plywood ½″ × 16″ × 16″ (11 mm × 40 cm × 40 cm)

B. Screws and wing nuts, 2 required: buy plated (non-rusting) ones. The length will depend on the thickness of the table top. Dome-topped screws are easier to clean.

C. Sheet of rigid plastic for surface.

Instructions for Work Surface

1. Glue plastic sheet C to board A.
2. Drill holes for screws 2″ (5 cm) in from sides and 2″ (5 cm) in from the back of board A.
3. Drill holes in table top 4″ (10 cm) from front edge.
4. Fix work surface to table, allowing an overlap of about 4″ (10 cm).

Shopping List for An Underneath Work Surface (Example sizes.)

A. Board: plywood ½″ × 16″ × 16″ (11 mm × 40 cm × 40 cm)

B. Sides, 2 required: softwood ⅝″ × 2″ × 6″ (14 mm × 5 cm × 15 cm). The width of the sides determines how low the work surface will be.

C. Sheet of rigid plastic for surface.

Instructions for Underneath Work Surface

1. Glue plastic sheet C to board A.
2. Fix sides B to board A with non-rusting wood screws.
3. Carefully drill table so that the screws will be in the center of sides B and 1¼″ (3 cm) from each end.
4. Paint or stain sides B and fix to table with long non-rusting screws.

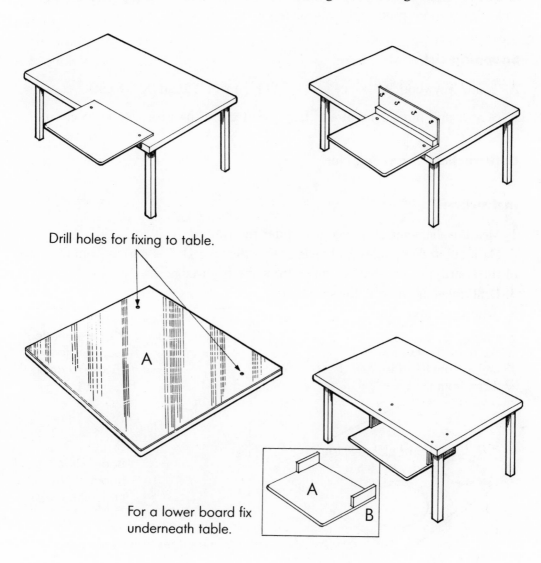

Drill holes for fixing to table.

For a lower board fix underneath table.

Mixing Board

This board will hold a mixing bowl firmly while you are mixing all types of ingredients with a spoon, a hand mixer, or an electric hand held mixer. If a hard-plastic-topped board is used it is better to have the holes cut professionally with an electric jigsaw, but if you do the job use a fine blade to help prevent chipping. Cut edges can be protected by applying an edging strip.

Shopping List

A. Board: plywood ½″ × 14″ × 14″ (11 mm × 35 cm × 35 cm)

B. Screws and nuts, 2 required: dome-headed are the easiest to keep clean

Construction: Screw and Nut

Instructions

1. Measure diameter of bowls just under the rim.
2. Mark out and cut holes for bowls so that they are 1½″ (4 cm) in from the sides of the board and the same distance from the front edge.
3. Drill holes in board A for screws.
4. Sandpaper and paint.

Make screw holes about 1¼″ (3 cm) in from the sides and 3″ (7.5 cm) from the back.

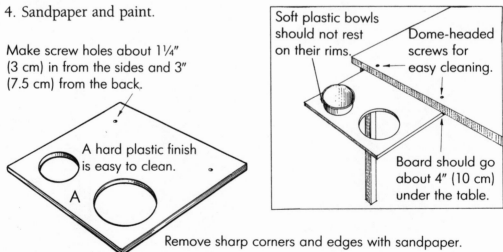

A hard plastic finish is easy to clean.

A

Soft plastic bowls should not rest on their rims.

Dome-headed screws for easy cleaning.

Board should go about 4″ (10 cm) under the table.

Remove sharp corners and edges with sandpaper.

Shoe And Boot Remover

This small aid will give a little more independence and save that struggle when trying to get the shoes off—and an even greater struggle when rubber boots are involved. The "V" shaped cut-out may have to be made bigger if it is to be used for getting off very large sizes. (If desired, a batten can be added at the heel edge to prevent the foot slipping.) Instead of shoelaces, you can use a soft, rounded elastic which allows pulling the shoe on and off without tying the laces.

Shopping List

A. Board: softwood ¾" × 5¼" × 16" (19 mm × 13.5 cm × 40 cm)

B. Riser: softwood ¾" × 2" × 5¼" (19 mm × 5 cm × 13.5 cm)

C. (Optional: softwood batten 1" × 1" × 5¼" (25 mm × 25 mm × 13.5 cm))

Construction: Glue and Nail

Instructions

1. Cut out board A as illustrated.
2. Fix riser B so that it does not touch the "V" cut-out.
3. Sandpaper till smooth and remove all sharp corners and edges.
4. (Optional: Fix on a heel stop batten.)

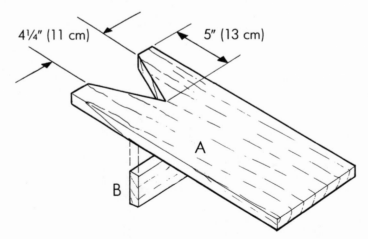

4¼" (11 cm)   5" (13 cm)

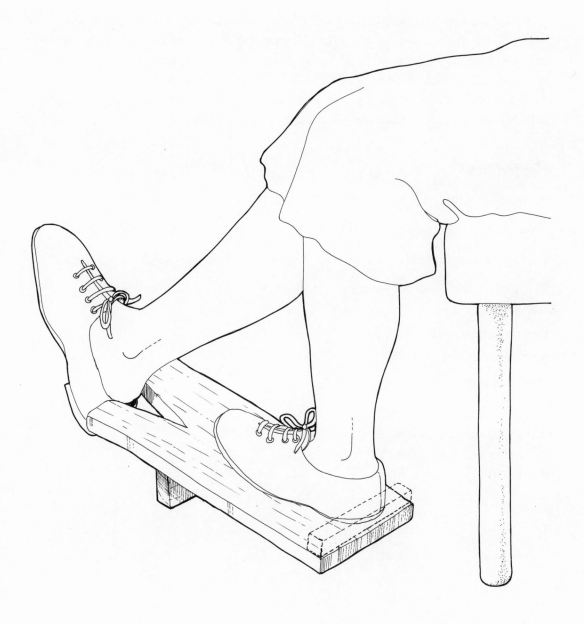

Hobby Work Top

As we grow older the garage and the garden shed seem to be too cold to work in once the summer comes to an end. It is possible to do some work or enjoy a hobby using the kitchen table if you make a hobby work top. The size of the working area can be made larger or smaller, depending on the kind of work you want to do. Should you wish to fix a vise to the work top, make the table edge batten wide enough to take the vise clamp. See illustration.

Shopping List

A. Base: plywood ⅜″ × 18″ × 25″ (8 mm × 45 cm × 62.5 cm)

B. Table edge: softwood 1″ × 1″ × 25″ (25 mm × 25 mm × 62.5 mm)

C. Top edge: softwood ½″ × 2″ × 25″ (11 mm × 5 cm × 62.5 cm)

D. Sides, 2 required: softwood ½″ × 2″ × 4″ (11 mm × 5 cm × 10 cm)

Construction: Glue and Nail

Instructions

1. Fix table edge B to base A.
2. Fix top edge C to base A.
3. Cut an angle on sides D.
4. Fix sides D to base A.

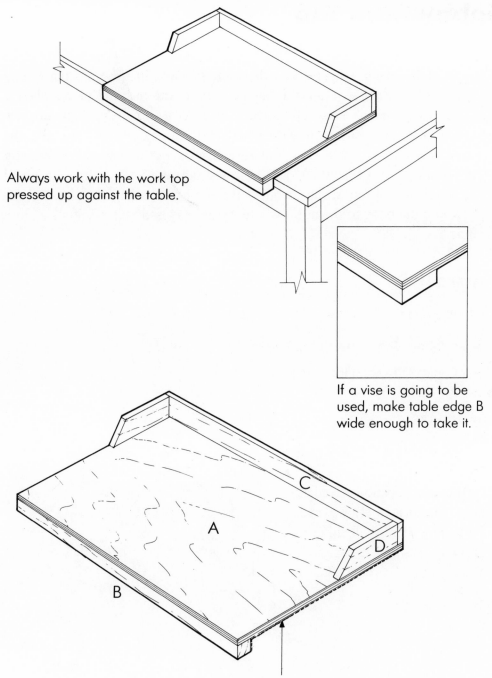

Always work with the work top pressed up against the table.

If a vise is going to be used, make table edge B wide enough to take it.

C

A

B

D

For added protection, glue cloth to base A.

Aprons

An apron, tailor-made, with pockets the right size and in the right place, will make it possible to move around the home with all the bits and pieces needed while keeping the hands free. Carefully design the size and shape of the pockets so that the hands can easily get into them, and at the same time make sure that the articles to be carried will fit and not fall out when the person bends over. Several aprons should be made and used for various purposes. (If desired, to avoid having to tie the apron strings, you can extend one string long enough to come around the body to the front, where it can be closed with a self-stick cloth fastening.)

Shopping List

A. Cloth: example size only 24″ × 28″ (60 cm × 70 cm)

B. Cloth tapes: about 2 yards (2 meters)

C. (Optional: self-stick cloth for fastening)

Instructions

1. Measure the person and make pattern.
2. Cut out cloth A and hem edges.
3. Sew on pockets. Don't make them too big or they will fall open.
4. Sew on tapes.

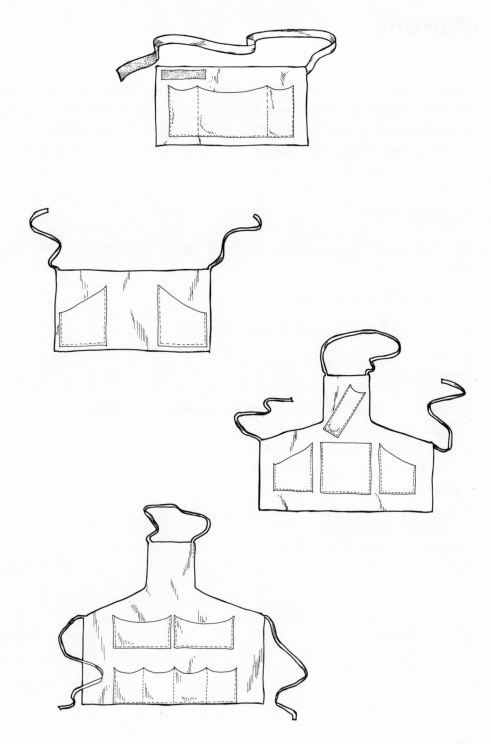

Bandolier

Those who do not want to be cluttered up with an apron may find the bandolier a better option for use indoors and in the garden. Any size of pocket can be made, and if the angle is right, no difficulty will be found in using them.

The bandolier must be made left- or right-handed and the length will depend on the size of the person who is to wear it.

Shopping List

A. Cloth: canvas or strong cloth. Size for three pockets 10" × 25" (25 cm × 62.5 cm)

B. Hook: bent from stiff wire

C. Ring: small curtain ring, or bend from stiff wire

Instructions

1. Fold cloth in half lengthwise and mark out three pockets.
2. Cut the angle of the pockets.
3. Sew pocket sides and bottoms.
4. Cut the ends to a point and sew.
5. Fix string and hook to top end.
6. Fix ring to lower end.
7. Adjust string length.

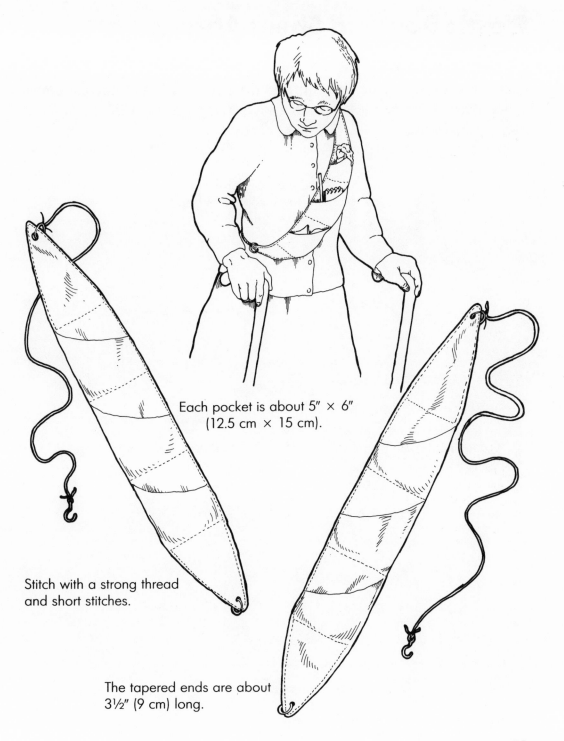

Each pocket is about 5″ × 6″
(12.5 cm × 15 cm).

Stitch with a strong thread
and short stitches.

The tapered ends are about
3½″ (9 cm) long.

Plastic Bag and Sheet Aprons

Plastic aprons can be quite expensive, but these are cheap enough to be "throw aways". Pockets can be stuck on with good quality insulation tape.

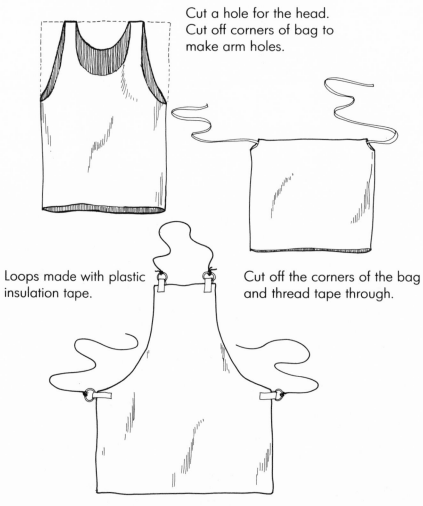

Cut a hole for the head.
Cut off corners of bag to
make arm holes.

Cut off the corners of the bag
and thread tape through.

Loops made with plastic
insulation tape.

Cut out shape from plastic sheet.

DINING ROOM AND LIVING ROOM

The living room or the sitting area of the dining/living room must be made draft free, warm, and light. It is not always easy to achieve, but every effort has to be made if you are really to enjoy your leisure hours. Drafts seem to invade a room from the most unlikely places, but they have to be found. After checking windows and doors, look for places where pipes may come through the floor and, while on your knees, make sure cold air is not coming up through any gaps between the boards.

Don't leave carpets down which do not lie perfectly flat on the floor. If there are badly worn edges and threadbare patches which could trip you, try turning the carpet around so that they are hidden under furniture, or in places where you do not walk. Don't polish under carpets and mats. Get an electrician to install another electrical outlet in a higher, easier-to-reach place, and fix a hook to hold the looped cord.

Don't put loose mats on polished floors.

Have all doors and windows made draft-free.

Modify the buffet if necessary.

Sit in a good light.

Big wheels are needed on thick carpets.

Carpet wall-to-wall for warmth.

Some Ideas for Wooden Chair Modifications

There are many modifications which can be made to wooden dining and kitchen chairs which will help you to sit more comfortably at the table with the rest of the family. The following series of drawings shows some of the things that can be done with ⅜″ (8 mm) plywood. It is important to get a kitchen chair modified, as most of the food can then be prepared while sitting down.

As most wooden chairs are made from a hardwood it will be necessary to drill pilot holes for the screws.

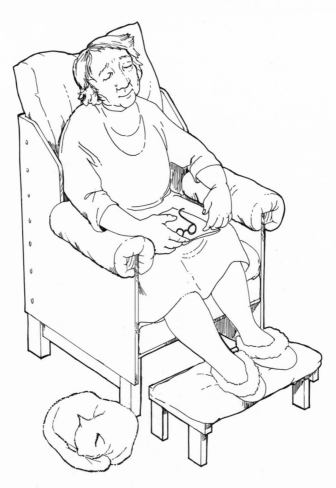

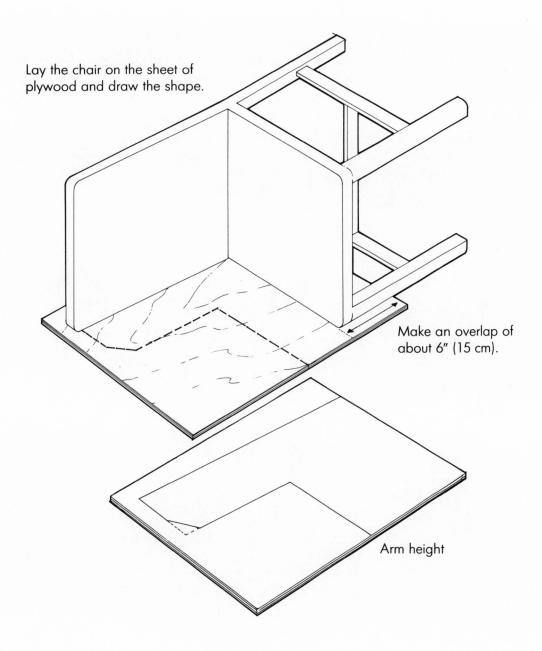

Lay the chair on the sheet of plywood and draw the shape.

Make an overlap of about 6″ (15 cm).

Arm height

Remove all sharp
corners and edges.

Fix on the arms.

Screw the sides
to the chair.

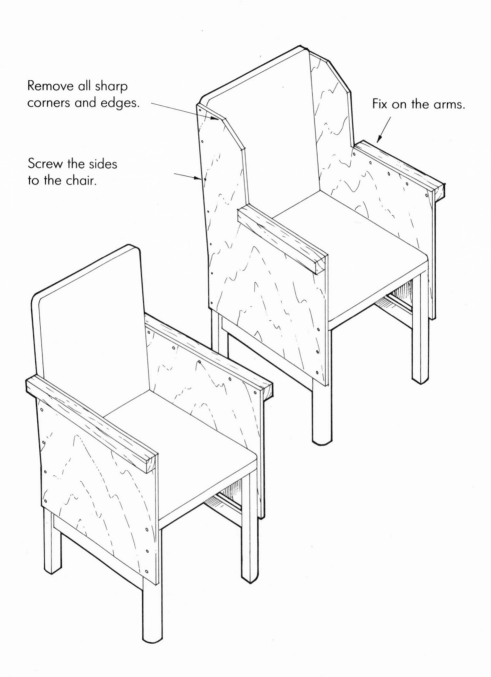

Make a loose cloth cover for back.

Width to fit chair.

Ask your medical adviser to give you the height and thickness for the foam cushion.

Foam cushion glued or tied to plywood.

The back can be tied or screwed in position. Attach it at the angle suggested by the medical adviser.

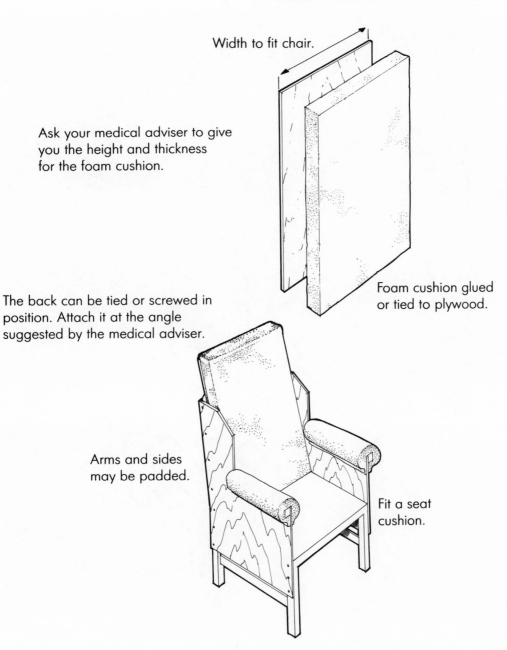

Arms and sides may be padded.

Fit a seat cushion.

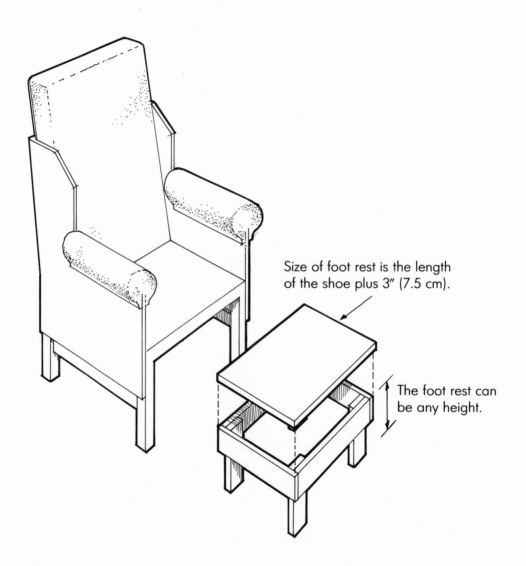

Size of foot rest is the length
of the shoe plus 3″ (7.5 cm).

The foot rest can
be any height.

Wheeled Chair With Arms

Every effort must be made to make it possible for all the family to sit down together for meals, and this can often be done by installing self-locking casters, so a chair can be wheeled. If it has to be pushed over very thick carpets, buy larger casters. They should have shafts which fit into a hole drilled in the chair legs, and be self-locking.

Note: This chair is safe to use only on carpeted, unslippery floors.

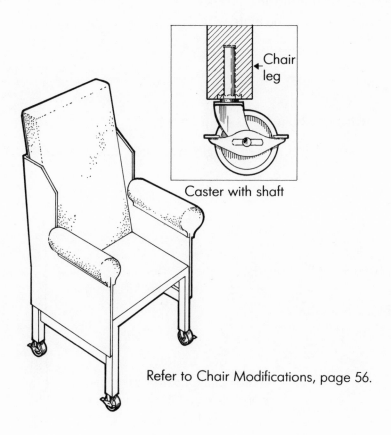

Caster with shaft

Refer to Chair Modifications, page 56.

Chair and Table Raisers

There is no good reason why you have to live with chairs and tables which are too low. They can all be raised to a better height by making the legs longer with raising blocks. So long as they fit well and do not let the furniture feel insecure by even the slightest wobble, they will be used. Two types are illustrated—one can be fitted to wood or metal furniture, but the other can only be used on wooden legs. Tubular steel chairs and tables can often be altered in height by buying metal tube which will just push over the leg. This tube can be cut to length, fitted over the existing leg, drilled, and held in place by self-tapping screws. It is not possible to give any dimensions as these must be taken from the furniture and the height must be suggested by the medical adviser. Remember that the fit must be very good and do not make them too high, which would cause the furniture to become unstable.

Shopping List

A. The box: hardwood about ¾″ (19 mm) thick

B. Blocks: softwood. These must fit snugly in the box. Don't forget that 4 are required.

Instructions

1. Measure the leg.
2. Cut the plywood as illustrated.
3. Make the box.
4. Cut the block B to size.
5. Sandpaper and paint.

The extension tube should be a good fit.

To protect the floor fit the same type of tips as used on walking canes.

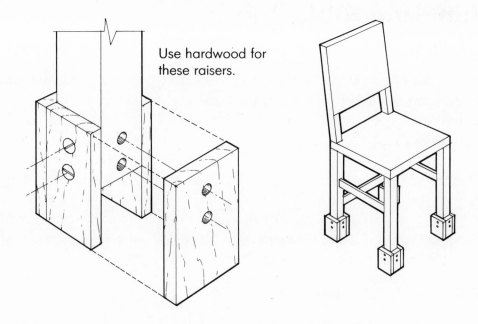

Use hardwood for these raisers.

As a table is not moved very often the raisers do not have to be fixed to the legs.

This box is a sliding fit.

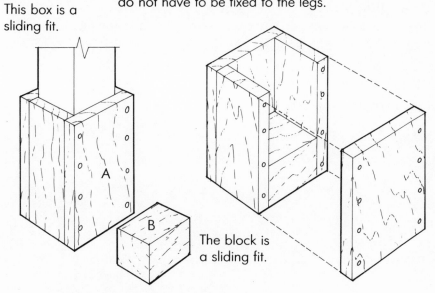

A

B

The block is a sliding fit.

The height of the block determines the height the table will raise.

Draft Screen

Screens do not have to be very tall and heavy, especially if you are always going to be sitting down while being protected from drafts.

Shopping List for Each Panel

A. Uprights, 2 required: softwood 1½″ × 1½″ × 5 ft (4 cm × 4 cm × 1.5 m)

B. Dowels, 2 required: ½″ (12 mm) diameter × 16″ (40 cm)

C. Hinges, 2 required. Ordinary hinges will do, but double action are better, as the panels can then be swung through 180°.

D. Screen covers: cloth or plastic

Instructions

1. Drill holes in uprights A 1¼″ (3 cm) from each end for dowels B.
2. Glue dowels B into uprights A. Lay on flat surface while the glue dries.
3. Fix the hinges C 2″ (5 cm) from each end.
4. Sandpaper and paint.
5. Join panels together.
6. Fix on screen covers with a stapler.

For garden use, fit hooks for guy ropes.

There are many types of hinges available.

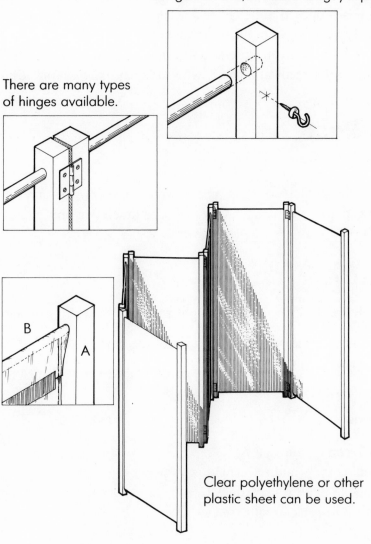

B

A

Clear polyethylene or other plastic sheet can be used.

The Favorite Armchair

The armchair is one piece of furniture one grows to love, and over the years it seems to become more comfortable; the thought of it being replaced by something which is supposed to be better does not bear thinking about. The next few pages give details of how an older armchair can be modified, in the hope that it will become an even greater friend and not have to be taken away. Discuss the problem with your medical adviser, who may have some more ideas.

Back Rest

This aid is only suitable for those chairs which have loose, heavy cushions, as it fits underneath them. Armchairs vary in size so much that only a materials list can be given.

Shopping List

A. Back: plywood ¼" (6 mm) × height required × width of back cushion

B. Cloth: strong piece of cloth the width of the back A × 14" (35 cm)

C. Strings, 2 lengths required: strong cord about 2 yards (2 meters)

Instructions

1. Cut off 2 corners of back A.
2. Round all corners and edges with sandpaper.
3. Sew loops to cloth B for strings C.
4. Fix cloth B to back A with contact glue.
5. Fix strings to cloth B.
6. Put back A in chair at the required angle and tie to chair feet as illustrated.
7. Replace cushions.

Sew on loops or use eyelets.

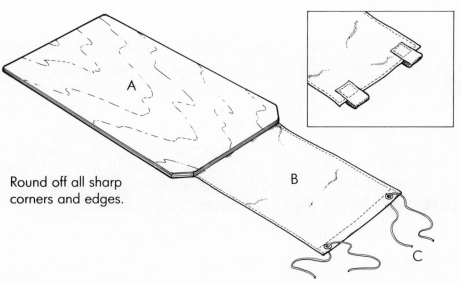

A

Round off all sharp
corners and edges.

B

C

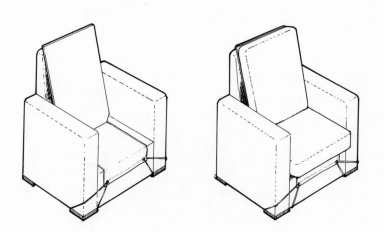

Leg Rest

Ask your medical adviser which height and angle are best for the leg to be kept at. Solid wood is better to use than plywood as it is less likely to bend under your weight.

Shopping List

A. Rest: softwood, minimum size ¾″ × 6″ × length (19 mm × 15 cm × length). To calculate length, add together length of rest required to hold leg, plus a minimum of 8″ (20 cm) which will be under the cushion.

B. Support: softwood, minimum size ¾″ × 6″ × height required (19 mm × 15 cm × height)

C. Batten: softwood 1½″ × 1½″ × 6″ (4 cm × 4 cm × 15 cm)

Construction: Glue and Nail

Instructions

1. Fix batten C to support B.
2. Fix support B to rest A.
3. Sandpaper and paint or stain.
4. Upholster rest A.

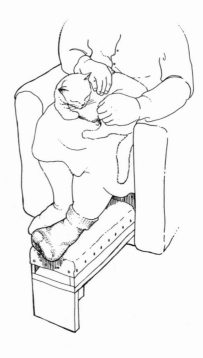

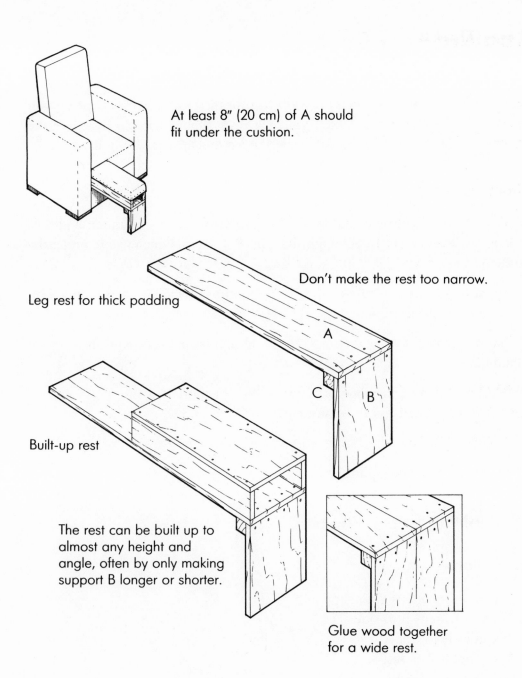

At least 8" (20 cm) of A should fit under the cushion.

Don't make the rest too narrow.

Leg rest for thick padding

A

C

B

Built-up rest

The rest can be built up to almost any height and angle, often by only making support B longer or shorter.

Glue wood together for a wide rest.

Shaped Leg Rest

This is another version of the leg rest which your medical adviser may prefer you to use. The upholstery on which your leg rests should completely cover the woodwork, so that there is no danger of the leg touching anything hard.

Shopping List

A. Rest: ½″ (11 mm) plywood or ¾″ (19 mm) softwood × minimum width 6″ (15 cm) × length of leg to be supported, plus 8″ (20 cm) which will fit under the cushion

B. Support: ½″ (11 mm) plywood or ¾″ (19 mm) softwood × minimum width 6″ (15 cm) × height required

C. Support batten: softwood 1½″ × 1½″ × 6″ minimum (4 cm × 4 cm × 15 cm minimum)

D. Sides, 2 required: plywood or softwood ½″ (11 mm) × about 4″ (10 cm) × the length of leg that has to be supported

E. Side battens, 2 required: softwood 1″ × 1″ (25 mm × 25 mm)

F. Cloth and foam for upholstery

Construction: Glue and Nail

Instructions

1. Fix support battens C to support B.
2. Fix side battens E to sides D.
3. Fix sides D to rest A.
4. Fix support B to rest A.
5. Sandpaper and paint.
6. Fix upholstery between sides D as illustrated.

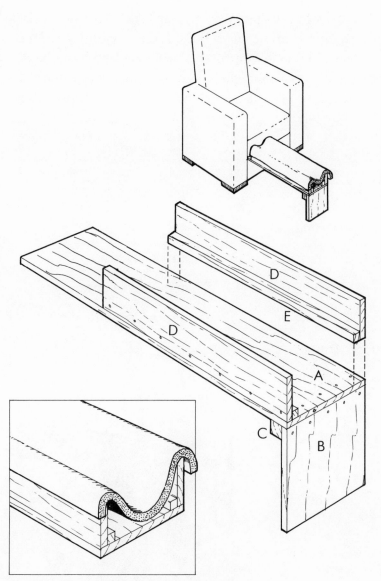

Cloth and foam fixed between sides D.

Leg Rest Extension

If you have one of these, you can "put your feet up" whenever you feel like it. There is no need to fix the rest to the chair, but if it does tend to move it can always be tied to the chair's foot with a cord. The angle and length can be decided by your medical adviser, after which it will be possible to work out all the dimensions. Foam upholstery can be bought from some stores cut to the exact size you want.

Shopping List

A. Top: plywood ¼″ (6 mm)

B. Sides, 2 required: plywood ¼″ (6 mm)

C. Side batten long, 2 required: 1″ × 1″ (25 mm × 25 mm)

D. Side batten front, 2 required: 1″ × 1″ (25 mm × 25 mm)

E. Side batten back, 2 required: 1″ × 1″ (25 mm × 25 mm)

F. Back: plywood ¼″ (6 mm)

G. Front: plywood ¼″ (6 mm)

H. Foam or other upholstery material

I. Cloth to cover padding

Construction: Glue and Nail

Instructions

1. Work out all the dimensions.
2. Cut out sides B.
3. Fix side battens long C to top edge of sides B.
4. Fix side battens front D to sides B.
5. Fix side battens back E to sides B.
6. Fix back F to assembled sides B.
7. Fix front G to assembled sides B.
8. Fix top A to sides.
9. Sandpaper and paint or stain.
10. Upholster top A.

Side—2 required.

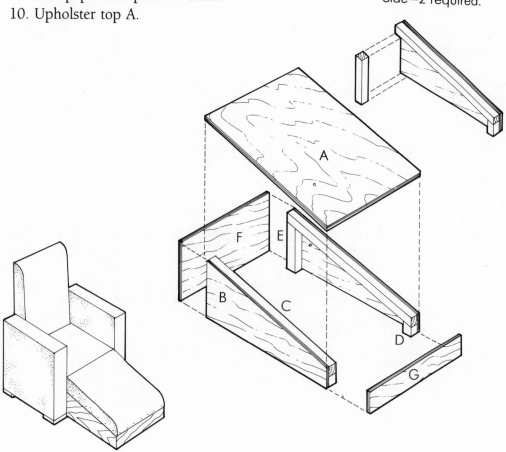

Armchair Tray

This tray fits close to the body and is held in place by two self-stick cloth tapes. It can very quickly be removed in an emergency.

Shopping List

A. Tray: plywood ¼″ (6 mm) × 18″ (45 cm) × width of chair plus 4″ (10 cm)

B. Sides, 2 required: softwood ½″ × 2″ × 18″ (11 mm × 5 cm × 45 cm)

C. Tray edge: softwood ½″ (11 mm) × 2″ (5 cm) × width of chair plus 4″ (10 cm)

D. Self-stick cloth

Construction: Glue and Nail

Instructions

1. Make cut out if required.
2. Fix sides B to tray A so they extend an inch or so beyond outside of chair arms.
3. Fix tray edge C to tray A.
4. Sandpaper and paint.
5. Place on chair and find best position for self-stick cloth tapes. (See illustration.)
6. Make self-stick cloth the right lengths, and glue to best position on sides B and matching places on armchair.

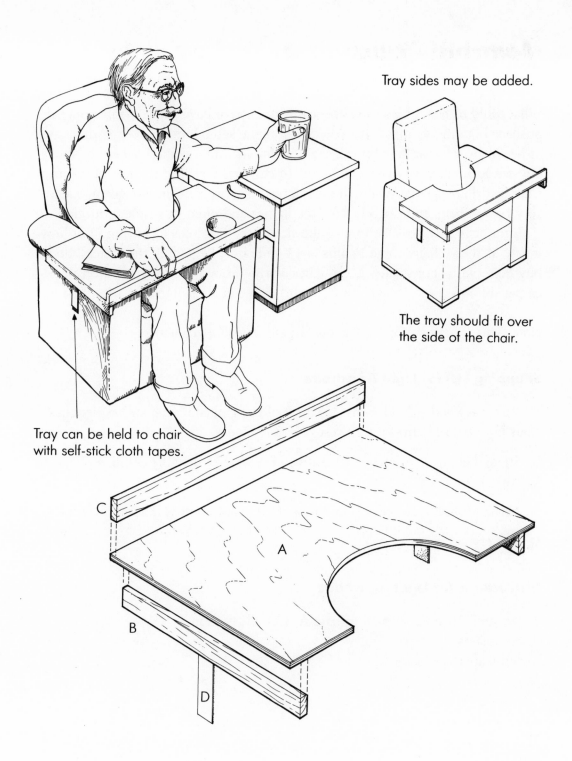

Tray sides may be added.

The tray should fit over the side of the chair.

Tray can be held to chair with self-stick cloth tapes.

C

A

B

D

Movable Armchair or Trolley

What could be better than to be able easily to push or have your favorite armchair pushed about the room, so that you can sit in the sun on those lovely spring days or be able to get that little bit closer to the fire as winter comes. Where possible, buy self-locking, large casters, about 2″ (5 cm) and install in the feet of the arm chair by drilling a hole. Where this is not possible, two versions are given, one for very heavy chairs and the other for the lighter and often more modern ones.

Again, it is only possible to give the size of the materials to buy and not how much, as these chairs come in all shapes and sizes. Regarding the casters, don't buy those with very small wheels, particularly if they have to be used on thick-carpeted floors. Wheels of about 2″ (5 cm) diameter are suitable for most homes.

Note: This is only suited for use on carpeted, unslippery floors.

Shopping List for Light Armchairs

A. Base: plywood ½″ (11 mm) × width of chair plus 3″ (7.5 cm) × length of chair plus 10″ (25 cm) for foot rest plus 3″ (7.5 cm)

B. Strengthening strip, 2 required: softwood ¾″ × 2″ × length (19 mm × 5 cm × length)

C. Chair stops, 8 required: battens 1″ × 1″ × 3″ (25 mm × 25 mm × 7.5 cm)

D. Casters

Instructions for Light Armchairs

1. Fix strengthening strips B to base A. (See illustration.)
2. Fix casters.
3. Sandpaper and paint.

Shopping List for Heavy Armchairs

A. Base: softwood ¾″ (19 mm) × width of chair plus 3″ (7.5 cm) × length of chair plus 10″ (25 cm) for foot rest plus 3″ (7.5 cm)

B. Cross timbers: softwood ¾″ (19 mm) × 6″ (15 cm) × width of chair

C. Chair stops, 8 required: battens 1″ × 1″ × 3″ (25 mm × 25 mm × 7.5 cm)

D. Casters

Instructions for Heavy Armchairs

1. Make base A with softwood planks. (See illustration.)
2. Fix casters.
3. Put chair on trolley and mark out where feet battens have to be fixed.
4. Fix feet battens.
5. Sandpaper and paint.

½″ (11 mm) plywood

Trolley for a light armchair

Fix wooden battens around feet to stop chair moving while being pushed along.

Trolley for a heavy armchair

Trolley Table

This table is of similar construction to others in this book, but to stop it slipping off, two little wooden dowels peg it to the trolley. A range of holes is drilled, so that the table can be placed either closer to you or further away.

The height and width will depend on the size of the chair and the person sitting in it, and this you must find out yourself. Try and make your armchair a real living center and have several tables all fitted out for various activities.

Shopping List

A. Tray: plywood ½" × 14" × length (11 mm × 35 cm × length). (Have this length extend an inch or two past B on each side.)

B. Sides, 2 required: plywood ⅜" × 12" × height (8 mm × 30 cm × height)

C. Side battens, 2 required: softwood 1½" × 1½" × 12" (4 cm × 4 cm × 30 cm)

D. Front: plywood ⅜" × 4" × length (8 mm × 10 cm × length). The front must not restrict leg movement but must be as deep as possible to give sides maximum strength.

E. Front battens, 2 required: softwood 1½" × 1½" × 4" (4 cm × 4 cm × 10 cm)

F. Dowels, 4 required: wooden dowel ¼" diameter (6 mm) × 1" (25 mm) long

Instructions

1. Carefully work out all the dimensions for the table.
2. Fix side battens C to sides B 1½" (4 cm) in from edge. (See illustration.)
3. Fix front battens E to front D.
4. Drill holes in bottom of sides B for dowels F, ½" (12 mm) from each end.
5. Glue in dowels F. (See illustration.)
6. Fix sides B to front D.
7. Fix top A to assembled sides B and front D.
8. Sandpaper and paint or stain.

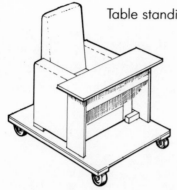

Table standing on light trolley

The table must fit over
any chair fixings.

Table standing on heavy trolley

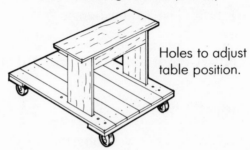

Holes to adjust
table position.

Side B

1½" (4 cm)
from the
end.

C

B

Drill holes
for dowels.

Front D

D   E

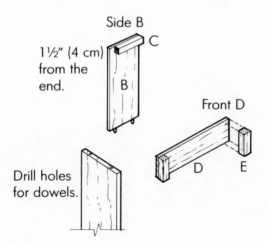

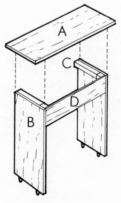

A

C

D

B

Make D as
deep as
possible.

Dowels ½" (12 mm) long

79

Tilting the Armchair

Your medical adviser may prefer you to sit in a chair which is at a slight angle. This can be done by making small angled blocks as illustrated. With the chair tilted back, your feet will be further away from the ground and a foot rest may be needed to let you sit comfortably.

Shopping List

A. Blocks: plywood or wood off-cuts about 4″ × 4″ × height (10 cm × 10 cm × height) to give required angle

Construction: Glue and Screw

Instructions

1. Glue pieces of wood together to make blocks A.
2. Remove casters, if applicable.
3. Cut the glued wood to shape and angle for blocks A.
4. Fix blocks A to front feet of chair.
5. Check for stability and, if the chair seems likely to tip back under normal use, make a stabilizing board as illustrated.
6. Sandpaper and paint or stain.

Glue plywood off-cuts together.

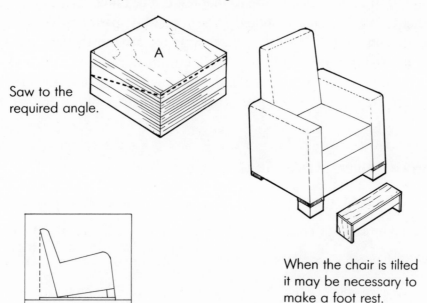

Saw to the required angle.

When the chair is tilted it may be necessary to make a foot rest.

To determine length of stabilizing board, align with the top of the backrest.

Stabilizing board

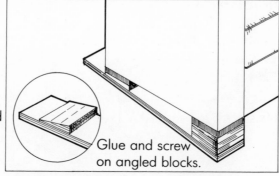

Glue and screw on angled blocks.

If the chair is unstable when tilted, cut a wedge and screw it with a length of thick plywood for the full depth, to a line projected vertically to the top of the backrest.

Angled Foot Rest (For Armchair Sitting)

When reclining in an armchair an angled foot rest can be much more comfortable and relaxing than a flat one. It should be well padded, particularly where the heels rest. In cold weather a small blanket wrapped around the feet will keep them nice and warm in their little box. Work out the angles by resting the person's feet on cushions. The sizes given in the shopping list are only intended as a guide, because the size of the feet play a big part in the size of the finished foot rest.

Shopping List (Adjust measurements as appropriate.)

A. Boards, 2 required: plywood $\frac{3}{8}''$ × 8″ × 12″ (8 mm × 20 cm × 30 cm)

B. Sides, 2 required: plywood $\frac{3}{8}''$ × 8″ × 8″ (8 mm × 20 cm × 20 cm)

C. Battens: softwood 1″ × 1″ × 6″ (25 mm × 25 mm × 15 cm)

Construction: Glue and Nail

Instructions

1. Mark out angles on sides B as illustrated.
2. Fix battens C to boards A.
3. Fix sides B to boards A.

The angles required are
drawn on the sides B.

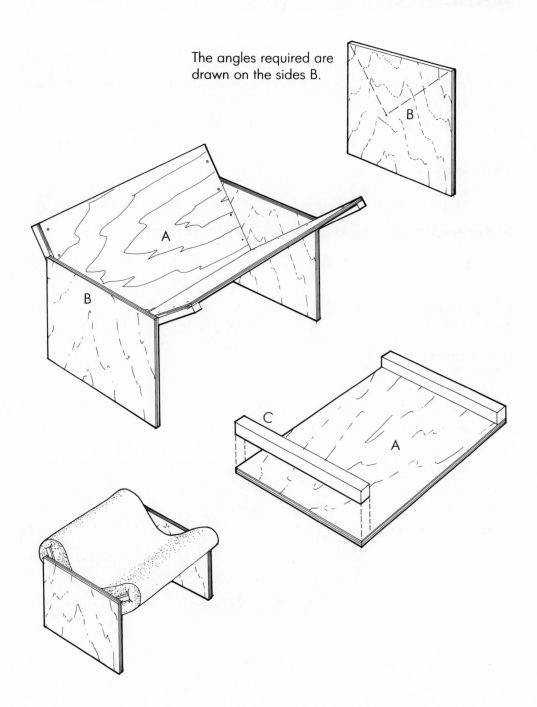

Book Rest

A book rest can be made to fit any armchair or bed table, whatever its size. To hold a heavy book soon tires the strongest of us, so a book rest is a must for the avid reader.

To obtain the preferred angle, measure it while the person is reading a book.

Shopping List

A. Board: plywood ¼″ × 10″ × 12″ (6 mm × 25 cm × 30 cm)

B. Angle brackets, 2 required: softwood ½″ × 6″ × 8″ (11 mm × 15 cm × 20 cm)

C. Rest: softwood ½″ × 1¼″ × 12″ (11 mm × 4 cm × 30 cm)

Construction: Glue and Nail

Instructions

1. Find the preferred angle.
2. Cut wood angle brackets B as illustrated.
3. Fix angle brackets to board A.
4. Fix rest C ½″ (12 mm) from the bottom.
5. Sandpaper and paint.

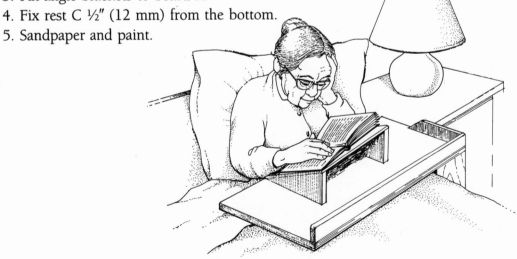

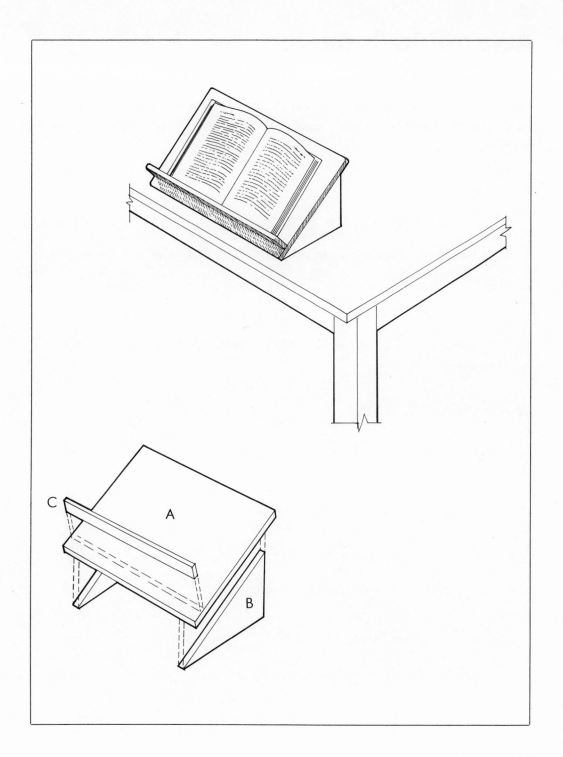

Adjustable Book Rest

This is almost as easy to make as the fixed version—apart from the fact that a book can be held at almost any angle, it has the advantage that it will fold flat for traveling.

Shopping List

A. Board: plywood ¼″ × 10″ × 12″ (6 mm × 25 cm × 30 cm)

B. Board side, 2 required: softwood ½″ × 1¼″ × 10″ (11 mm × 3 cm × 25 cm)

C. Legs, 2 required: ½″ x 1¼″ × 10″ (11 mm × 3 cm × 25 cm)

D. Rest: softwood ½″ × 1¼″ × 12″ (11 mm × 3 cm × 30 cm)

E. Wing nuts and bolts, 2 required: about ¼″ diameter × 1½″ (6 mm diameter × 4 cm long)

Construction: Glue and Nail

Instructions

1. Drill holes in sides B and legs C for wing nuts and bolts E.
2. Cut off corners of sides B as illustrated.
3. Fix sides B to board A.
4. Fix rest D to board A 1″ (25 mm) from the bottom.
5. Sandpaper all parts and paint.
6. Fix legs C to sides B with screws and wing nuts.

The board can be made any size, adjusted to any angle, and locked in position by a wing nut.

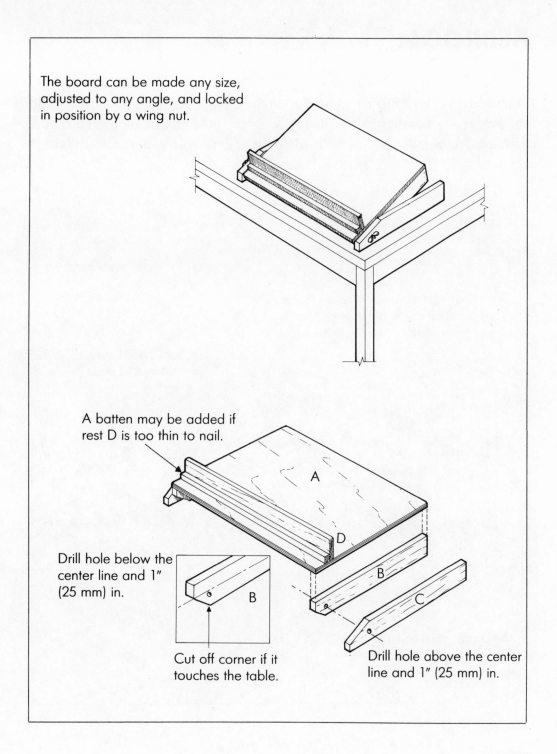

A batten may be added if rest D is too thin to nail.

A

D

Drill hole below the center line and 1" (25 mm) in.

B

B

C

Cut off corner if it touches the table.

Drill hole above the center line and 1" (25 mm) in.

BEDROOM

Reading in bed or having to get up during the night mean that good lighting and an easily reached switch are essential. The various little modifications to furniture described in the following pages should only be done with your medical adviser's approval.

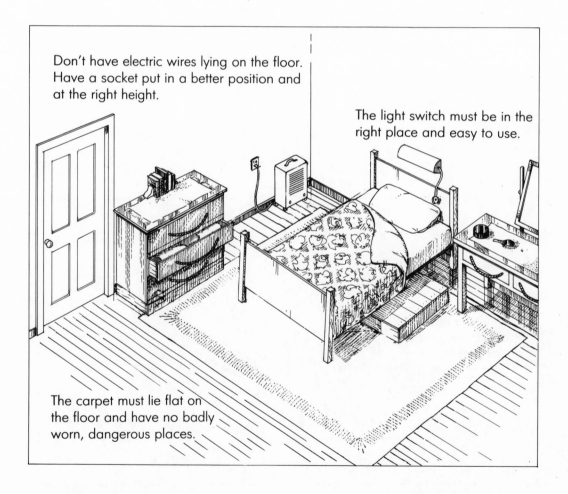

Don't have electric wires lying on the floor. Have a socket put in a better position and at the right height.

The light switch must be in the right place and easy to use.

The carpet must lie flat on the floor and have no badly worn, dangerous places.

Chest of Drawers

The drawers in some old chests are heavy. If they do not open easily, have them attended to before thinking about any changes. Should you feel that changing the knobs will be of no help, tie a piece of soft rope between them. This will let you pull the drawer open with your hands at their most comfortable distance apart. And if you need to use only one hand the drawer will open smoothly if the center of the rope is pulled.

Shopping List

A. Length of soft rope. When calculating this measurement, don't forget to allow for the knots.

Instructions

Tie the rope between the knobs, but do not stretch it too tightly, as it will then be too close to the drawer and hard to grasp.

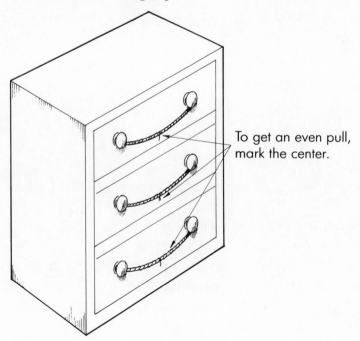

To get an even pull, mark the center.

Plinth for a Chest of Drawers

Some of the older chests of drawers are very heavy and would need a strong plinth, while the newer ones, often made of plywood and other manufactured materials, can safely be placed on a much lighter structure. All these chests, whether heavy or light, can become unstable if an open drawer filled with clothes is leant on. To overcome this problem, attach the chest to the wall with little brackets as illustrated.

Shopping List

A. Sides long, 2 required: ½″ (11 mm) × height required × length of chest plus 2″ (5 cm)

B. Sides short, 2 required: softwood ½″ (11 mm) × height required × depth of chest plus 2″ (5 cm)

C. Top: softwood ½″ (11 mm) × depth of chest plus 2″ (5 cm) × length of chest plus 2″ (5 cm)

D. Top corner battens, 4 required: softwood 1″ × 1″ × 3″ (25 mm × 25 mm × 7.5 cm)

Construction: Glue and Screw

Instructions

1. Fix sides A to sides B.
2. Fix top planks C to assembled sides A and B. For heavy chests, fix corner battens D.
3. Sandpaper, and paint to match chest.
4. Fix plinth to wall with metal brackets.
5. Place chest on plinth. Locate framing in wall so as to firmly anchor the screw, and fix chest to the wall with metal brackets.

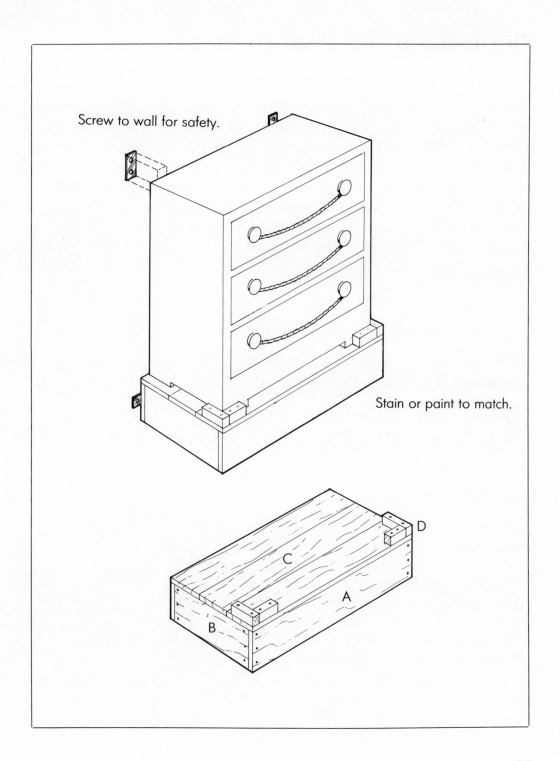

Screw to wall for safety.

Stain or paint to match.

C

D

A

B

Dressing Table Drawer Pull

Dressing table drawers are not usually heavy, but can be difficult to open by the knob, particularly if you also have a problem in getting your fingers around it. Two simple solutions are given which only take a few minutes to make. The rope does not have to be a piece cut off the clothes line; look for some colorful artificial silk rope, of the kind sometimes used for curtains. It comes in many colors and one may be found to match the room's décor. Marine supply stores also have soft nylon cord.

Shopping List for First Solution

A. Length of rope or thick cord

B. 2 eye screws

Shopping List for Second Solution

A. Length of rope or thick cord

B. Length of 1″ (25 mm) diameter dowel

Instructions

See illustrations.

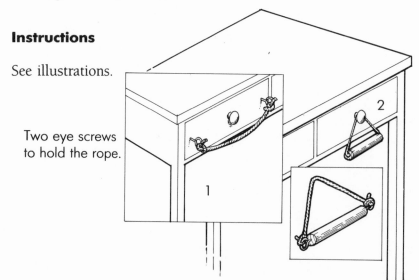

Two eye screws to hold the rope.

Drill 2 holes and glue in rope, or use eye screws. Tie rope around handle.

Bedside Cabinet

The bedside cabinet can be given a few little modifications to make it an even more useful piece of furniture. The illustration gives a number of these which will not take up much time or cost much money. Usually, removing the door and raising the cabinet up on a plinth are enough.

This edging will keep things from falling off.

To make it easier to open, fix a wooden stop at the back so that the drawer does not quite close.

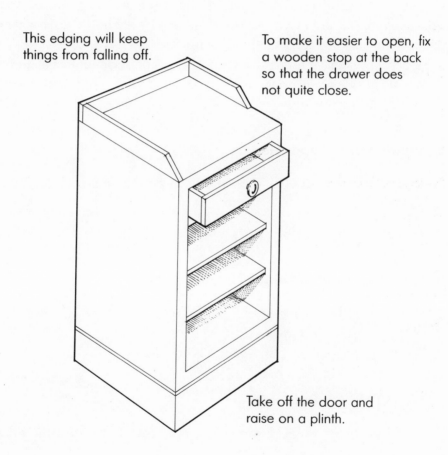

Take off the door and raise on a plinth.

Wardrobe

This may be a heavy piece of furniture with doors which are difficult to open and close. Get a handyperson in to make all the adjustments that you need, and at the same time to do any other alterations to it which will make life easier for you. If it has now become a problem to reach up to get clothes off the rod, have it lowered. But before doing this try a long-handled reacher, as illustrated. If ladies do not like hanging their dresses on a low rod, a long reacher must be used. Heavy items such as overcoats and rainwear should be kept by the house door where they can dry without making other clothing damp.

Modern glues make it possible to fix all sorts of wooden, metal, and plastic fittings to the inside of the door, and these can be placed where you can easily reach them. Various hooks, rods, and shelves are available in all sorts of sizes.

Shopping List for Door Hooks

A. Board: softwood ½″ (11 mm) × 2″ (5 cm) × measure the door for this dimension

B. Hooks: a wide range of shapes and sizes is available

Instructions for Door Hooks

1. Mark out for hooks and screw holes if required.
2. Drill holes and fix screws.
3. Finish by sandpapering and painting or staining.

Shopping List for Door Rod

A. Board: softwood ½″ (11 mm) × 2″ (5 cm) × measure the door for this dimension

B. Sides, 2 required: softwood ½″ × 2″ × 3″ (11 mm × 5 cm × 7.5 cm)

C. Rod: wooden dowel ½″ (11 mm) × length to suit

Instructions for Door Rod

1. Drill sides B for rod C.
2. Drill board A for sides B.
3. Fix sides B to board A with glue and screws.
4. Fix rod C to sides B with glue.
5. Finish by sandpapering and painting or staining.

Shopping List for Clothes Rod

A. Ends, 2 required: softwood ½″ × 2″ × 3″ (11 mm × 5 cm × 7.5 cm)

B. Rod: wooden dowel about 1″ (25 mm) diameter × length to suit

Instructions for Clothes Rod

1. Mark out ends A for rod and screws.
2. Drill holes for screws.
3. Cut hole for rod with coping saw.
4. Fix rod B into ends A with glue.
5. Finish by sandpapering and painting or staining.

Shopping List for Long Reacher

A. Handle: wooden dowel about 3 feet (1 meter) long
B. Hook: one very large hook which can be bent to shape

Instructions for Long Reacher

1. Drill pilot hole for hook half the diameter of the screw.
2. Bend screw roughly to shape.
3. Fit screw into handle. Remove the hook from the handle for any reshaping.

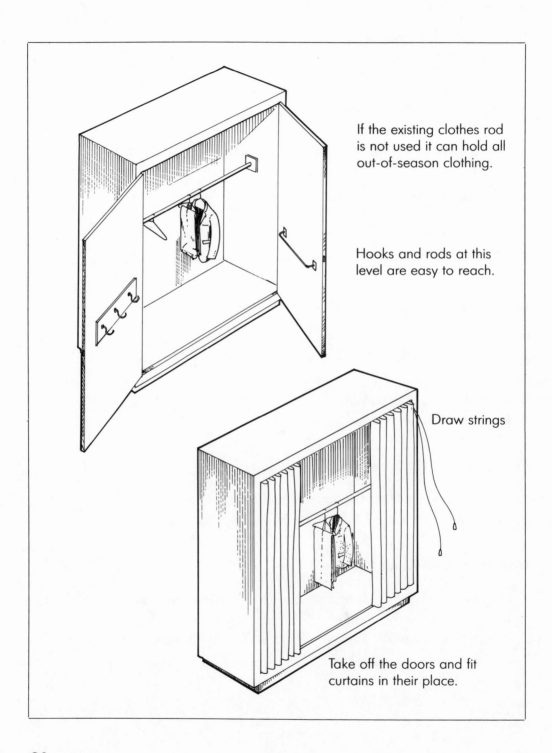

If the existing clothes rod
is not used it can hold all
out-of-season clothing.

Hooks and rods at this
level are easy to reach.

Draw strings

Take off the doors and fit
curtains in their place.

DOOR HOOKS

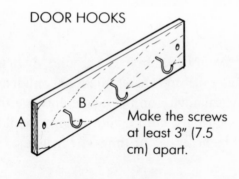

A
B

Make the screws at least 3″ (7.5 cm) apart.

The length of A will depend on the width of the door.

DOOR ROD

Allow enough clearance around the rod.

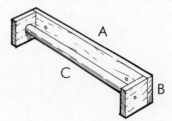

A
C
B

Drill above rod, providing space for screwdriver.

CLOTHES ROD

A metal supporting hook must be fitted for rods over 5′ (1.5 m) long.

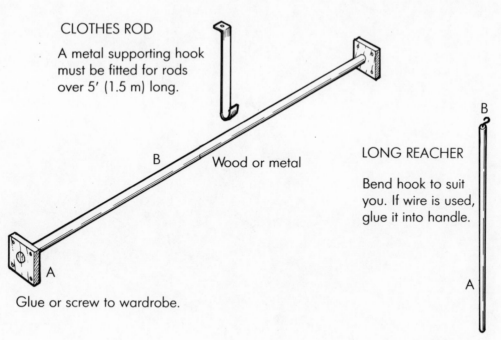

B   Wood or metal

A

Glue or screw to wardrobe.

LONG REACHER

Bend hook to suit you. If wire is used, glue it into handle.

B

A

Cut to length after testing.

Bedside Step

A bedside step effectively reduces the height your bed is from the ground. By first stepping onto the box you should feel much safer and therefore more confident about getting into and out of bed. Get medical advice on the height and size to make the step. It is not possible to give dimensions, but the illustrations should be studied. For stability, the width should be at least four times the height.

These are the dimensions required.

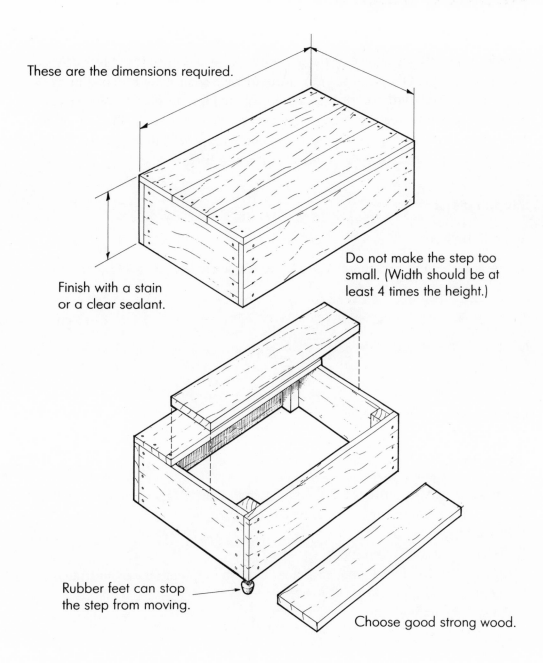

Finish with a stain
or a clear sealant.

Do not make the step too
small. (Width should be at
least 4 times the height.)

Rubber feet can stop
the step from moving.

Choose good strong wood.

99

Bedding Support

Some discomfort may be felt by the pressure of the bedding on the feet, particularly when lying on the back with the toes pressing against well-tucked-in sheets and blankets. This little support holds up the bedding to give the feet freedom from this pressure. See the illustration for how it is placed in the bed. Guide dimensions only are given as the thickness and width of the mattress may make it necessary to increase the height and width of the back.

Shopping List

A. Back: plywood ⅜″ × 18″ × 20″ high (8 mm × 45 cm × 51 cm high)

B. Top and base, one of each: plywood ⅜″ × 10″ × 18″ (8 mm × 25 cm × 45 cm)

C. Battens, 2 required: softwood for bottom batten 1½″ × 1½″ × 18″ (4 cm × 4 cm × 45 cm). Top batten 1½ × 1½ × 17¼″ (4 cm × 4 cm × 43 cm).

D. Braces, 2 required: plywood ⅜″ × appropriate height, or use corners cut from A or B

Construction: Glue and Nail

Instructions

1. Cut off corners as illustrated and sandpaper all sharp edges so that they will not damage the bedding. It is better to round the corners.
2. Fix battens C to back A.
3. Fix base and top B to back A.
4. Add strength by fixing wooden braces D in the top corners as illustrated.
5. Thoroughly sandpaper.
6. Finish by painting.

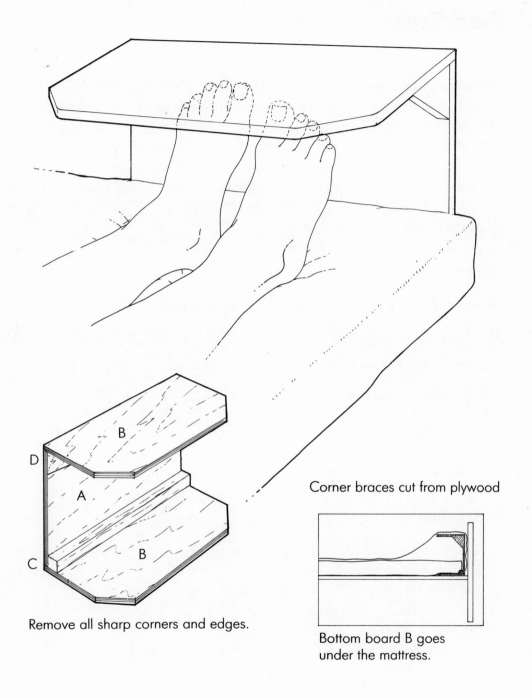

Remove all sharp corners and edges.

Corner braces cut from plywood

Bottom board B goes
under the mattress.

101

Bed Tray

Being comfortable while sitting up in bed for any length of time is not an easy thing to achieve, but with a well-designed back rest and a bed tray which is the right size and height, it is possible to overcome at least some of the problems. If, after searching the stores, the right tray cannot be found, the one illustrated here is easy to make and will not cost very much. Do not hesitate to change any or all of the dimensions, as this is the only way to get the most suitable bed tray for you. (This tray can be designed to fit a favorite armchair, as well. Refer to the Armchair Tray, on page 74.)

Shopping List

A. Tray: plywood $\frac{3}{8}$″ × 10″ × 30″ (8 mm × 25 cm × 75 cm)

B. Sides, 2 required: plywood $\frac{3}{8}$″ × 10″ × 12″ (8 mm × 25 cm × 30 cm)

C. Front edge: softwood $\frac{3}{8}$″ × 1″ × 29¼″ (8 mm × 25 mm × 74.6 cm)

D. Side edge, 2 required: softwood $\frac{3}{8}$″ × 1″ × 10″ (8 mm × 25 mm × 25 cm)

E. Batten, 2 required: softwood 1″ × 1″ × 10″ (25 mm × 25 mm × 25 cm)

Construction: Glue and Nail

Instructions

1. Cut sides B as illustrated and round the corners.
2. Fix battens E to sides B.
3. Fix sides B to tray A 1½″ (4 cm) from each end.
4. Cut the corners off side edges D.
5. Fix edge C and edges D to tray A.
6. Sandpaper thoroughly so that no damage can be done to bedding.
7. Finish by painting.

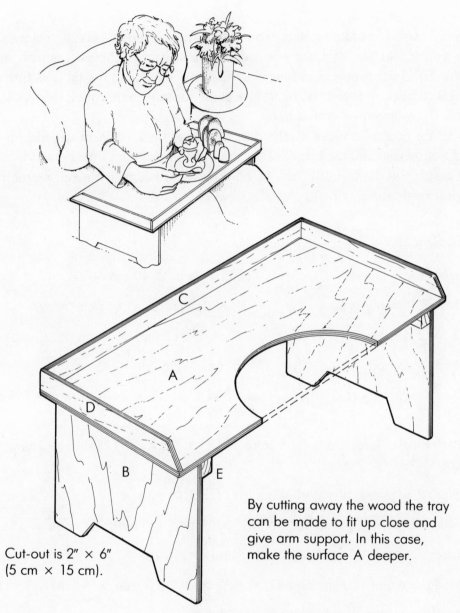

Cut-out is 2" × 6"
(5 cm × 15 cm).

By cutting away the wood the tray
can be made to fit up close and
give arm support. In this case,
make the surface A deeper.

Remove all sharp corners and edges.

Bed Table for Hobbies

This bed table is extra wide and extra strong and, although heavy, it does give a firm working surface to those who would like to occupy themselves with some hobby. For some people, a cut-out may have to be made in the table as this will allow it to fit close to the body and give some support to the arms; this is shown on the drawing with a dotted line.

It is not possible to give all the dimensions as some of them depend on the height of the bed and the height of the table top in relation to the person in a sitting position in the bed. It is easy to get these dimensions by measuring the person in exactly the way he or she would work.

Shopping List

A. Table top: plywood ⅜″ × 16″ × 24″ (8 mm × 40 cm × 60 cm)

B. Table edge long: softwood ½″ × 2″ × 24″ (11 mm × 5 cm × 60 cm)

C. Table edge short: softwood ½″ × 2″ × 8″ (11 mm × 5 cm × 20 cm)

D. Back: plywood ⅜″ × 16″ × 30″ (8 mm × 40 cm × 75 cm)*

E. Back bracket short, 2 required: softwood 1″ × 1″ × 14″ (25 mm × 25 mm × 35 cm)

F. Back bracket long, 2 required: softwood 1″ × 1″ × 30″ (25 mm × 25 mm × 75 cm)*

G. Side, 2 required: plywood ⅜″ × 8″ × 30″ (8 mm × 20 cm × 75 cm)*

H. Side battens, 4 required: softwood 1″ × 1″ × 6″ (25 mm × 25 mm × 15 cm)

I. Base: plywood ⅜″ × 16″ × 30″ (8 mm × 40 cm × 75 cm)

J. Skids, 2 required: softwood 1″ × 1½″ × 30″ (25 mm × 4 cm × 75 cm)

These dimensions must be measured by you.

Construction: Glue and Nail

Instructions

1. Make the assemblies A, D, G, and I as illustrated.
2. Fix sides G to back D.
3. Round the ends of skids J as illustrated.
4. Fix base I to complete back assembly.
5. Fix table to complete back assembly.
6. Finish by sandpapering and painting.

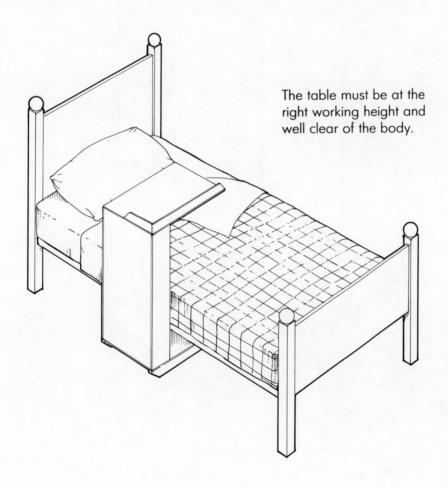

The table must be at the right working height and well clear of the body.

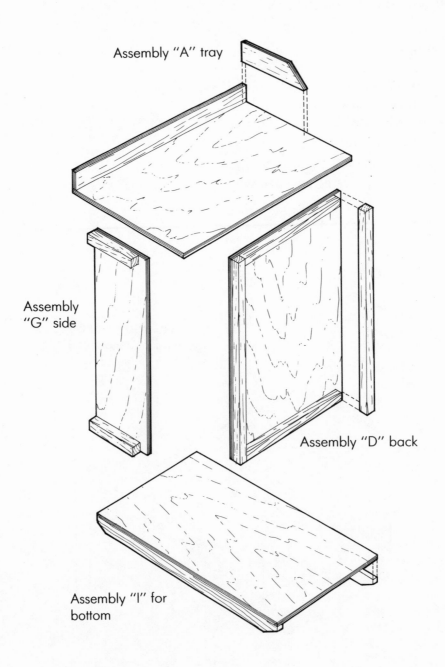

Assembly "A" tray

Assembly
"G" side

Assembly "D" back

Assembly "I" for
bottom

EXPLODED ASSEMBLY

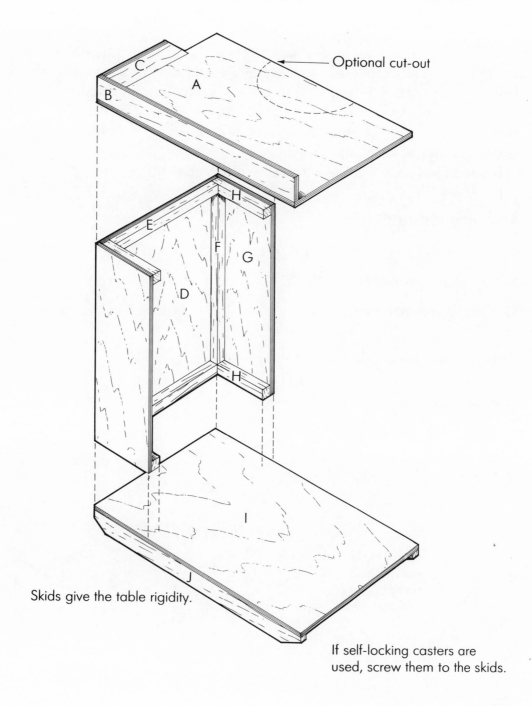

Optional cut-out

Skids give the table rigidity.

If self-locking casters are
used, screw them to the skids.

Ironing Board Bed Table

Not all ironing boards can be used for this purpose and some beds are too low. But you may be lucky and find this idea a quick and easy way of providing a bed table, although only as a temporary measure. Usually, the only suitable ironing boards are those of a wide modern design, as they are more stable. Besides going over the bed, they can be placed alongside it to make a long bed table, and when not needed can be folded up and put away.

If you do not want to make a tray, an ordinary tray can be used.

Shopping List for a Tray

A. Base: plywood ¼″ × 10″ × 14″ (6 mm × 25 cm × 35 cm)

B. Top edge: softwood ⅜″ × 2″ × 14″ (8 mm × 5 cm × 35 cm)

C. Sides, 2 required: softwood ⅜″ × 2″ × 7½″ (8 mm × 5 cm × 19 cm)

Construction: Glue and Nail

Instructions

1. Fix top edge B to base A.
2. Fix sides C to base A.
3. Finish by sandpapering and painting.

The ironing board must go over the bed far enough. Try it at various heights.

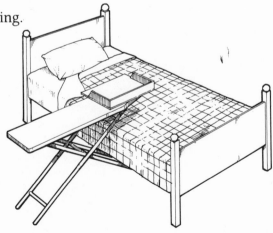

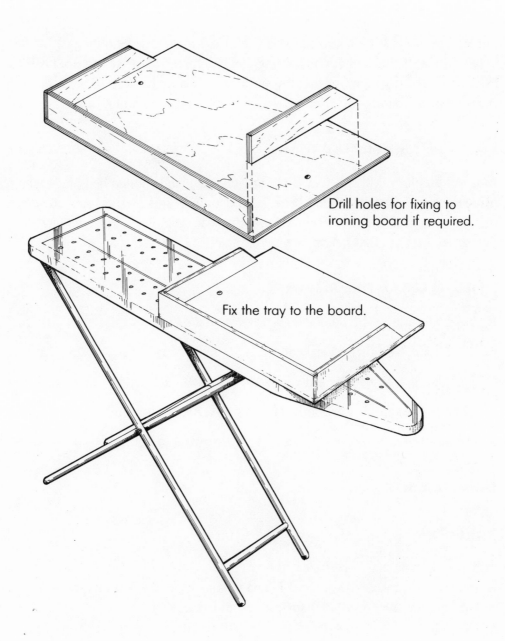

Drill holes for fixing to
ironing board if required.

Fix the tray to the board.

Bed Raisers

Three ways are given for how to raise a bed (to a maximum of 6 inches). By having this done, the task of others helping you will be made easier and not nearly so back-breaking. If you are having physiotherapy treatment, care must be taken to ensure that the bed is still strong enough to take the extra strain of the exercises.

Bed Raiser for Metal Bed Frames

As it is difficult to drill and fix wood or metal to a metal-framed bed, it is easier to place the legs in small wooden boxes as illustrated. This method can, of course, be used to raise all types of bed and is particularly suitable if a bed will have to be put back to its original height.

Shopping List for Four Raisers

A. Base, 4 required: hardwood ¾″ × 4″ × 4″ (19 mm × 10 cm × 10 cm)

B. Sides small, 8 required: hardwood ¾″ × 2½″ × 8″ (19 mm × 6 cm × 20 cm)

C. Sides large, 8 required: hardwood ¾″ × 4″ × 8″ (19 mm × 10 cm × 20 cm)

D. Blocks, 4 required: softwood to fit into box × height required, maximum 4″

E. Wood screws: No. 8 × 25 mm (1½″), 96 required

Construction: Glue and Screw

Instructions

1. Measure diameter of bed leg.
2. Determine dimensions of sides B and C, and base A. (See illustration.)
3. Drill and countersink holes for base A and sides C.
4. Drill pilot holes for screws in sides B half the diameter of the screws.
5. Fix sides B to sides C.

6. Fix assembled sides B and C to base A.
7. Sandpaper and stain or paint to match bed.
8. Cut blocks to size and fit into boxes.

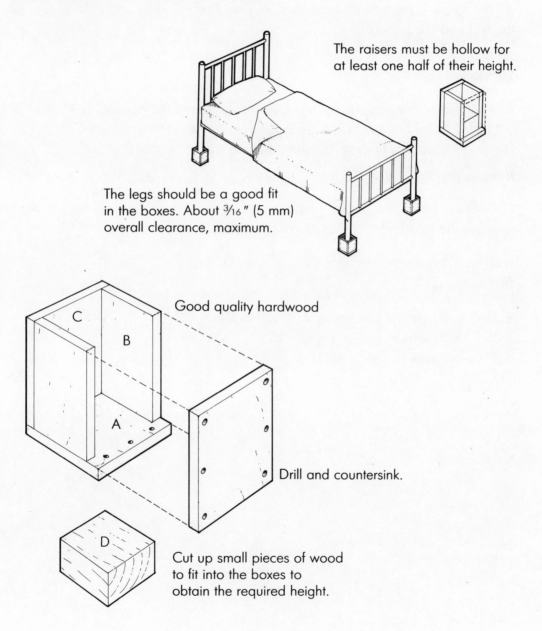

The raisers must be hollow for at least one half of their height.

The legs should be a good fit in the boxes. About $^3/_{16}$" (5 mm) overall clearance, maximum.

Good quality hardwood

Drill and countersink.

Cut up small pieces of wood to fit into the boxes to obtain the required height.

Wooden Bed Raiser for Wooden Framed Beds

This is a quick and effective way of raising a bed, but care must be taken in choosing the wood. It must be well seasoned and not liable to split under the weight of the bed and the person in it.

Shopping List

A. Four pieces of well seasoned wood about the size of the bed leg. The length is calculated by adding the height the bed has to be raised plus at least 6″ (15 cm). For heights over 6″, the overlap should equal the extension.

B. Nuts and bolts about ³⁄₁₆″ (5 mm) diameter, 8 required

C. Washers for above. These should be as large a diameter as possible to avoid splitting the wood when the nuts are tightened.

Instructions

1. Drill bed legs and extensions A to suit bolts.
2. Bolt extensions to bed legs.
3. Stain or paint to match the bed.

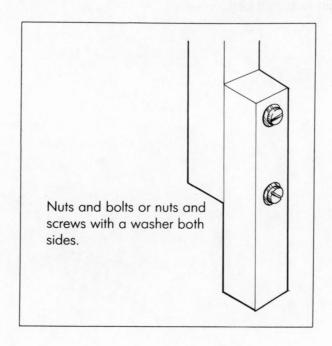

Nuts and bolts or nuts and screws with a washer both sides.

Metal Raiser for Wooden Bed Frames

Angle iron or angle aluminum makes a very strong leg and is quick to fit.

Shopping List

A. Four pieces of angle iron or angle aluminum. The length is calculated in the same way as for the wooden extension.

B. Nuts and bolts about ³⁄₁₆″ (5 mm) diameter, 16 required

C. Washers, large, 32 required

Instructions

1. Round all corners and edges of extenders A.
2. Drill bed legs and extenders A to suit nuts. Stagger the holes.
3. Bolt extenders to the bed.
4. Paint to match bed.

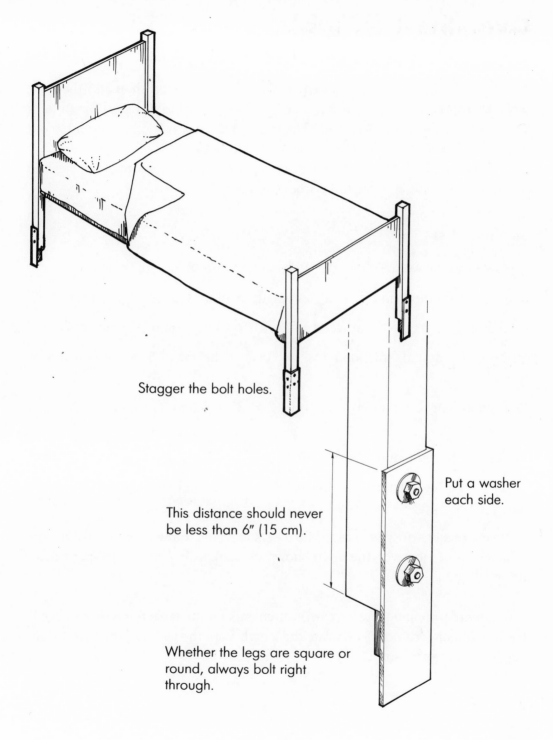

Stagger the bolt holes.

This distance should never be less than 6" (15 cm).

Put a washer each side.

Whether the legs are square or round, always bolt right through.

Over-the-Bed Table

This table can be made by a handyperson with a good workshop and the right tools. It must be well made, as it is a general purpose table and ideal for all hobbies or even making things for sale. There is no reason why it cannot be fitted out as a work bench with vise, electric sockets, and lighting.

To work out all the wood sizes, it is necessary to know the width of the bed and the height the table top has to be from the floor.

Shopping List

A. Table top: plywood $\frac{3}{8}$″ × 16″ × length (8 mm × 40 cm × length)

B. Back edge: softwood $\frac{3}{8}$″ × 2″ × length (8 mm × 5 cm × length)

C. Side edge, 2 required: softwood $\frac{3}{8}$″ × 2″ × 15$\frac{5}{8}$″ (8 mm × 5 cm × 39 cm)

D. Legs, 4 required: softwood 1$\frac{3}{4}$″ × 1$\frac{3}{4}$″ × height (4.5 cm × 4.5 cm × height)

E. Leg ties long, 2 required: softwood $\frac{1}{2}$″ × 3″ × length (11 mm × 7.5 cm × length)

F. Leg ties short, 2 required: softwood $\frac{1}{2}$″ × 3″ × 12″ (11 mm × 7.5 cm × 30 cm)

G. Lower leg ties, 2 required: softwood $\frac{1}{2}$″ × 3″ × 12″ (11 mm × 7.5 cm × 30 cm)

No instructions are given, as a skilled person would know how to make the traditional joints. However, the insert shows an alternative which anyone can make using lap joints.

Note: In order to find the correct measurements for the table top A, back edge B, legs D, and long leg ties E, calculate the length from the width of the bed and the height when the person is in bed.

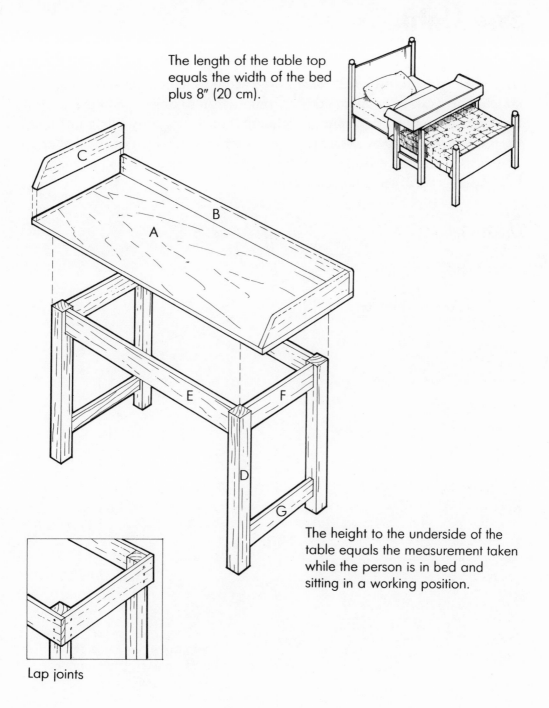

The length of the table top equals the width of the bed plus 8″ (20 cm).

C

B

A

E

F

D

G

The height to the underside of the table equals the measurement taken while the person is in bed and sitting in a working position.

Lap joints

Bed Light

It is very important that a light can be switched on and off by just reaching for a switch. There can be nothing more frightening than to wake up in the middle of the night and not be able to put the light on. If there is already a light fitted over the bed it may have to be altered to make it easy to use, and an example of this is illustrated. There is a wide choice of many types of lights and switches which are safe and easy to fit, including pull switches.

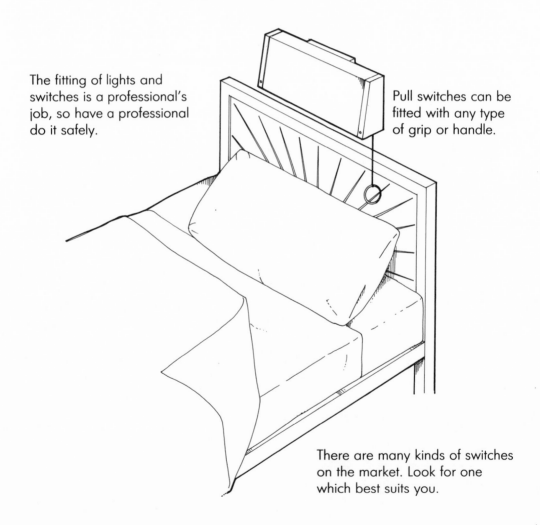

The fitting of lights and switches is a professional's job, so have a professional do it safely.

Pull switches can be fitted with any type of grip or handle.

There are many kinds of switches on the market. Look for one which best suits you.

BATHROOM

For an elderly person, the bathroom can be one of the most hazardous rooms in the house. The ideas suggested here will provide support where it is needed most—in getting into and out of the bath and in using the lavatory. Additional handrails fixed into the framing at strategic points can also make it easier to move about the room. (Refer to APPENDIX, page 178, for examples of standard available handrails.)

Note: Obtain the booklets on electrical safety in the home from local showrooms. Do not use electric appliances in the bathroom. Have any electrical installations checked regularly.

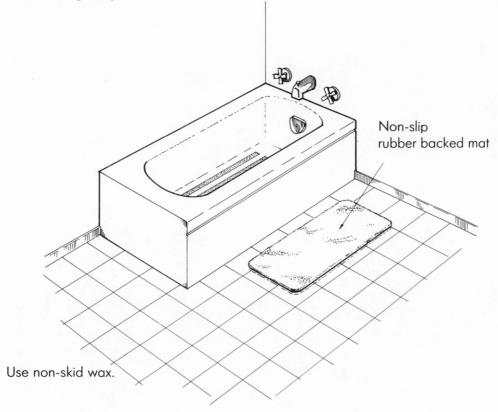

Non-slip rubber backed mat

Use non-skid wax.

Tiles and lino can be slippery when wet.

Overflow Bath Plug

By using a length of plastic tube instead of a plug, the water can never get too deep, because once the level reaches the top of the tube it runs away. For example, a 6″ (15 cm) length of tube will only allow the water to become about 5½″ (14 cm) deep. A smaller diameter pipe can be made to be a good push fit by winding plastic insulation tape around it.

A gentle push with the toe is usually enough to make the tube come out of the hole when you have finished bathing, but a length of cord or light chain can be fixed to the top of the tube so that it can be pulled out by hand.

Shopping List

A. Plug tube: semi-rigid plastic such as polyethylene

B. Plastic insulation tape

Instructions

Fit tube into plug hole by winding on insulation tape until a good push fit is achieved.

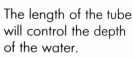

The length of the tube will control the depth of the water.

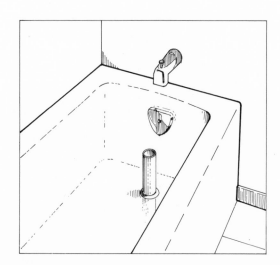

Bath Seat

If you use a wheelchair, this extended bath seat will help you to get from your chair to sit over the bath and back into the chair again. Some baths are made of plastic and tend to bend under pressure, making the fit of a seat important. (Refer to the APPENDIX for typical safe handrails.)

If you are able to get down into the bath but need a low seat, it is better to buy one, particularly if the bath is made of plastic.

Shopping List

A. Side: softwood ¾″ × 10″ × height from floor to top edge of bathtub (19 mm × 25 cm × tub height)

B. Seat: softwood ¾″ × 10″ (19 mm × 25 cm) × measurement from wall to outside edge of bathtub plus length of seat, usually about 10″ (25 cm)

C. Brackets, 2 required: plywood ⅜″ × 6″ × 6″ (8 mm × 15 cm × 15 cm) cut diagonally into 2

D. Batten short, 2 required: softwood 1″ × 1″ × 5″ (25 mm × 25 mm × 12.5 cm)

E. Batten long, 2 required: softwood 1″ × 1″ × 6″ (25 mm × 25 mm × 15 cm)

F. Side batten: softwood 1″ × 1″ × 7¼″ (25 mm × 25 mm × 18.5 cm)

G. Bath block: softwood 2″ × 2″ × 10″ (5 cm × 5 cm × 25 cm)

H. Dowels, 2 required: ¼″ diameter × 4″ (6 mm diameter × 10 cm)

I. Wall bracket: softwood ¾″ × 3″ × 14″ (19 mm × 7.5 cm × 35 cm)

Construction: Waterproof glue and non-rusting (galvanized) screws

Instructions

1. Fix battens D and E to bracket C.
2. Fix batten F to side A.
3. Fix assembled brackets C to side A.
4. Fix assembled side A to seat B.
5. Drill and fix dowels H into bottom of side A.
6. Cut wall bracket I to take seat B.
7. Shape bath block G to fit top of the bath side.
8. Fix wall bracket I to wall, anchoring it firmly to wall framing.
9. Drill 2 holes in the floor for dowels H about ½″ (12 mm) deep.
10. Place the assembled bath seat in position before fixing the bath block G to seat B, in order to get a good fit.
11. Sandpaper and give several coats of good quality paint.
12. Test thoroughly before use to make sure that it is a strong, rigid structure.

The seat can be fitted anywhere along the length of the bathtub.

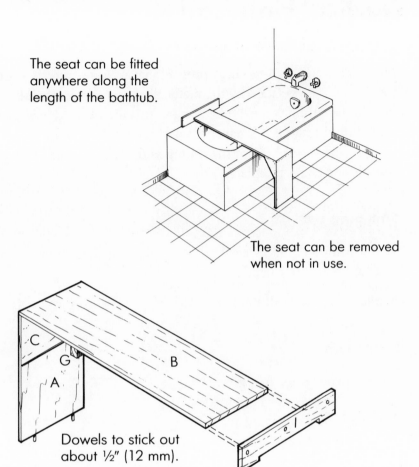

The seat can be removed when not in use.

Dowels to stick out about ½″ (12 mm).

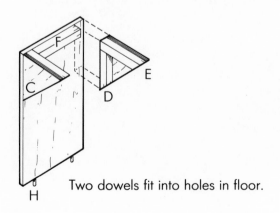

Two dowels fit into holes in floor.

Vertical Handrail

The vertical handrail requires professional welding and its position in the bathroom should be decided by the medical adviser. If your hands find it too difficult to hold the strong vertical tube because it is too big or dangerously slippery when held with wet hands, a smaller diameter one can be welded to it. As illustrated, it need not be vertical. Have the ceiling and floor checked to determine if they are suitable for fixing the plates.

Shopping List

A. Vertical tube: mild steel $1\frac{1}{2}''$ × height to ceiling (4 cm × height to ceiling). Test that it will not bend in use.

B. Plates, 2 required: mild steel $\frac{1}{8}'' \times 4'' \times 4''$ (3 mm × 10 cm × 10 cm)

Instructions

1. Drill plates B for fixing screws.
2. Cut tube A to exact length.
3. Weld tube A to center plates B.
4. Prepare surface of the metal for painting.
5. Finish with several coats of paint to guard against rust.
6. Firmly fix to floor and ceiling framing, which may require blocking.

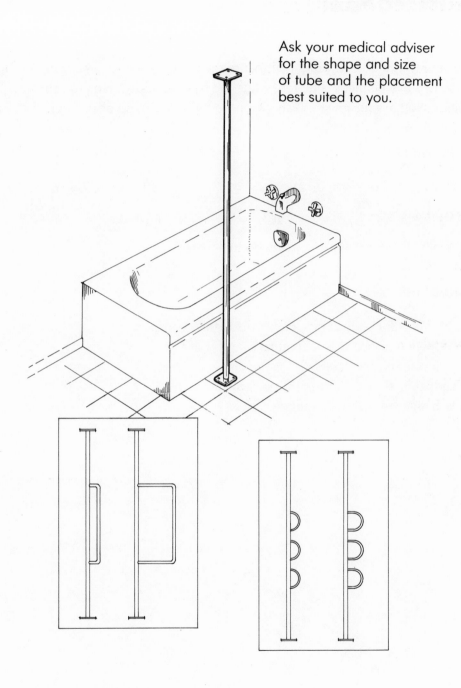

Ask your medical adviser
for the shape and size
of tube and the placement
best suited to you.

Bath Hanger

This is a little aid that a young member of the family can make as a school project. In fact two can be made, one for beside the bath, as illustrated, and the other for hanging clothes and towels away from the bath and fixed at the right height.

Shopping List

A. Board: wood or plywood about ½″ × 3″ × 12″ (12 mm × 7.5 cm × 30 cm)

B. Shelf: wood or plywood about ½″ × 3″ × 6″ (12 mm × 7.5 cm × 15 cm)

C. Hooks: large chrome-plated or plastic-coated hooks

Instructions

1. Drill holes for wall fixing screws through board A.
2. Fix shelf B to board A if required.
3. Mark out and fix hooks C.
4. Sandpaper smooth and paint or varnish.
5. Fix hanger to the wall framing.

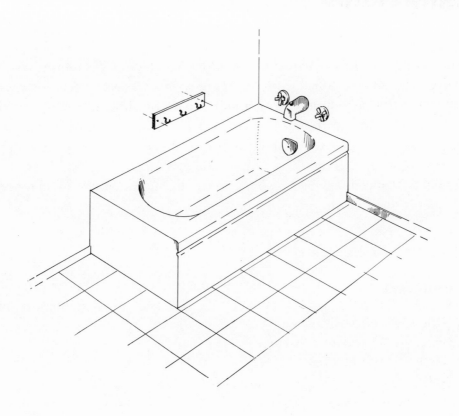

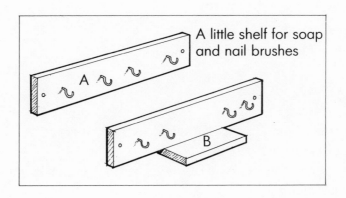

A little shelf for soap and nail brushes

A

B

Large Bathroom Platform

A large platform which gives plenty of room on which to manouver, and is also large enough to take a chair safely, can make it much easier to get into and out of the bath. The size will depend to a great extent on the floor space that can be used, but the width should not be less than 24" (60 cm). If it has to have a chair on it, this should be fixed to the platform with small metal brackets to prevent any risk of it slipping off. Even with a wide platform, it is a good idea to fix the chair if it has to be used as a support. The finished surface must be non-slip, whether it is wet or dry.

Shopping List (Example sizes.)

A. Top: exterior grade plywood thick enough not to bend under your weight. Plywood $\frac{1}{2}$" × 24" × length of tub (11 mm × 60 cm × length of tub). This will require extra support beneath.

B. Sides long, 2 required: softwood $\frac{5}{8}$" × 6" × length (14 mm × 15 cm × length)

C. Sides short, 2 required: softwood $\frac{5}{8}$" × 6" × 22$\frac{3}{4}$" (14 mm × 15 cm × 57 cm)

D. Corner battens, 4 required: softwood 1$\frac{1}{2}$" × 1$\frac{1}{2}$" × 6" (4 cm × 4 cm × 15 cm)

E. Small metal brackets, 4 required

Construction: Glue and Nail, using waterproof glue

Instructions

1. Assemble sides B and C using corner battens D.
2. Fix top A to assembled base.
3. Thoroughly paint. A non-slip surface must be used, even if it is only possible to put down rough matting.
4. Fix to floor with small metal brackets.

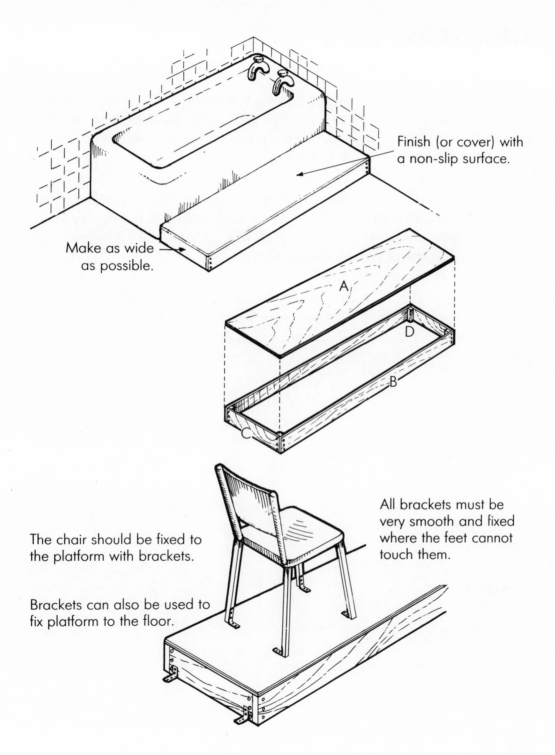

Finish (or cover) with a non-slip surface.

Make as wide as possible.

A

D

B

C

The chair should be fixed to the platform with brackets.

All brackets must be very smooth and fixed where the feet cannot touch them.

Brackets can also be used to fix platform to the floor.

129

Handrails

It is not always possible to buy a ready-made handrail which is exactly what is required, but this need not be a problem as they are not difficult to make. Welding can be done locally as most garages have the equipment; they will also be able to drill and countersink the holes. It is not essential to have the use of a pipe bending machine, as in most cases a butt joint is just as good for achieving the required shape. (However, to avoid sharp corners, pipes can be bent at a muffler shop.) Look at the illustrations for various ways of making handrails, but remember: no matter how good the rail is, it will be useless unless the wall and floor are strong enough to take the strain, so a careful examination by a professional is called for to determine how to fix the rails to the framing. As with the vertical handrail, other small metal tubes can be welded on to make it easier to hold. Make sure all welded joints are filed round and smooth before finishing. (Refer to the APPENDIX for examples of typical safe commercial grab bars.)

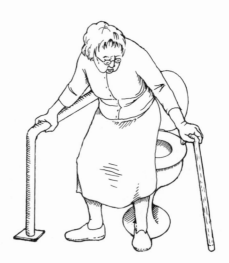

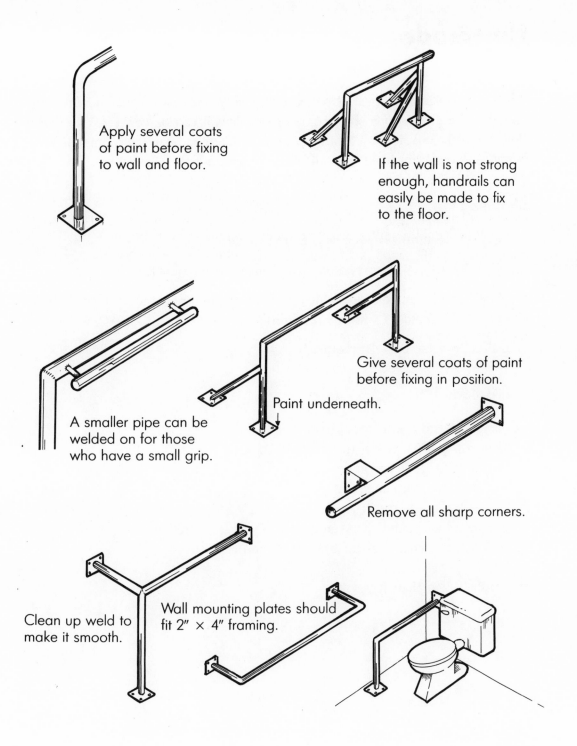

Apply several coats of paint before fixing to wall and floor.

If the wall is not strong enough, handrails can easily be made to fix to the floor.

A smaller pipe can be welded on for those who have a small grip.

Paint underneath.

Give several coats of paint before fixing in position.

Remove all sharp corners.

Clean up weld to make it smooth.

Wall mounting plates should fit 2″ × 4″ framing.

Commode

Try to find a steel frame chair which is not only the best height but also wide enough. The illustrations show some of the ways it can be converted so that it does not look conspicuous. If other people are likely to be in the room when it is being used, why not make a small screen to give a little privacy?

Shopping List

A. Seat: ⅜″ (8 mm) plywood × size to fit chair

B. Shelf: ⅜″ (8 mm) plywood × size to fit between chair legs

C. Shelf brackets, 4 required: angle iron or angle aluminum ⅛″ × 1″ × 1″ × 1″ (3 mm × 25 mm × 25 mm × 25 mm)

D. Self-tapping screws, 16 required

Instructions

1. Remove existing seat from chair.
2. Make a paper pattern of the shape of the hole.
3. Mark out the hole shape on seat A.
4. Cut out hole shape in seat A.
5. Drill screw holes in seat A.
6. Sandpaper and paint seat A and shelf B with polyurethane.
7. Drill holes in chair legs for brackets C and attach them.
8. Fix seat A to chair.
9. Fix shelf B to chair legs.

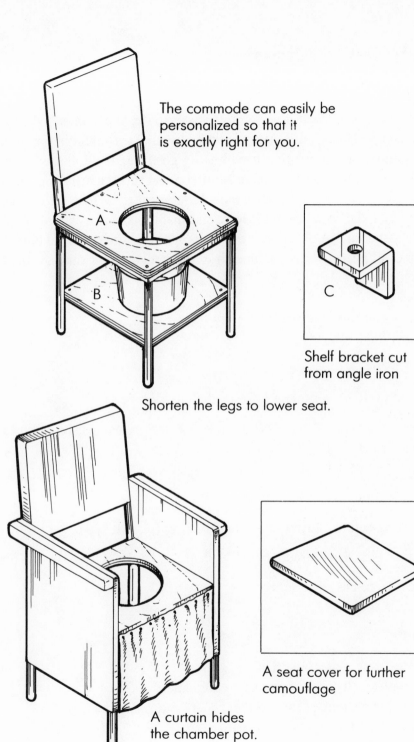

The commode can easily be personalized so that it is exactly right for you.

A

B

C

Shelf bracket cut from angle iron

Shorten the legs to lower seat.

A seat cover for further camouflage

A curtain hides the chamber pot.

Mobile Toilet Seat

The mobile toilet seat allows a person to transfer to the seat from a bed or a chair and be pushed to the lavatory, which can then be used without others being present. As a standard chair is used, it will easily go through the door and can be manouvered over the toilet. The choice of the metal tube chair is important as it must have no cross pieces which would hit the toilet. When the self-locking casters are fitted, the chair seat must have reasonable clearance over the top of the toilet (see illustration). A plastic seat can be bought and fitted instead of making a wooden one. (If necessary, a machine shop can drill and cut through the heavy metal for you.)

Note: Do not use this chair on a slippery floor.

Shopping List

A. Seat: plywood ⅜″ (8 mm) × size of the chair frame

B. Foot rest: plywood ⅜″ × 10″ (8 mm × 25 cm) × inside chair leg measurement less ¼″ (6 mm)

C. Angle irons, 2 required: ⅛″ × 1¼″ × 1¼″ (3 mm × 3 cm × 3 cm) × distance between front and back legs plus 10″ (25 cm)

D. Self-tapping screws, 11 required: non-rusting (plated) type

E. Nuts and bolts, 4 required: about ⅛″ diameter × ¾″ (3 mm × 20 mm)

F. Self-locking casters, 4 required

Instructions

1. Remove existing seat from chair.
2. Paint the metal chair frame with polyurethane.
3. Make a paper pattern of the hole and mark out on the seat A.
4. Cut the hole and round edge in seat A.

5. Drill holes for screws in seat A.

6. Sandpaper and paint with polyurethane.

7. Fix seat A to chair frame.

8. Fix self-locking casters to chair legs.

Instructions for Foot Rest

1. Drill chair legs for foot rest angle irons C.

2. Drill foot rest angle irons C so that holes line up with chair leg holes.

3. Paint foot rest angle irons C.

4. Fix foot rest angle irons C to chair legs.

5. Fix foot rest B to foot rest angle irons C.

6. Fix self-locking front casters to front of foot rest as illustrated.

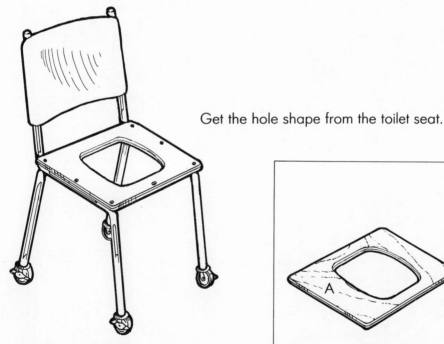

Get the hole shape from the toilet seat.

Choose self-locking casters which will fit up into the chair legs.

All edges and corners must be very smooth and rounded.

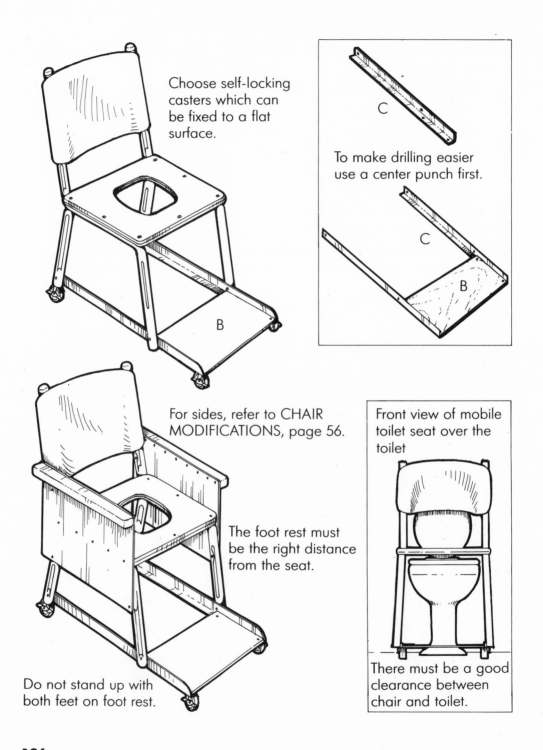

Choose self-locking casters which can be fixed to a flat surface.

To make drilling easier use a center punch first.

C

C

B

B

For sides, refer to CHAIR MODIFICATIONS, page 56.

The foot rest must be the right distance from the seat.

Do not stand up with both feet on foot rest.

Front view of mobile toilet seat over the toilet

There must be a good clearance between chair and toilet.

ENTRY, STAIRS, AND LANDING

Passages can be cold and drafty places, so make sure all the doors and windows fit well or have draft excluders. The exterior doors should be looked at very carefully, as this is where most of the cold air is coming from. Besides draft excluders, a heavy curtain can help a lot, and it will also cover the mail slot. These are jobs members of the family can do. They can also check for uneven and loose floorboards, carry out the wardrobe modifications to the hall clothes closet, and fit a safety security chain at the right height. For peace of mind, start fitting security locks to all downstairs windows and doors, and where necessary have those locks which are already there refitted so that they are easier to use. Have light switches placed close to the front door so that lights can be put on as the front door is opened.

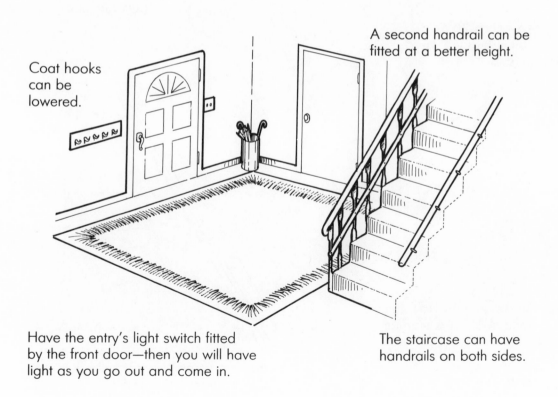

Coat hooks can be lowered.

A second handrail can be fitted at a better height.

Have the entry's light switch fitted by the front door—then you will have light as you go out and come in.

The staircase can have handrails on both sides.

Use heavy metal brackets, with all sharp corners and edges rounded.

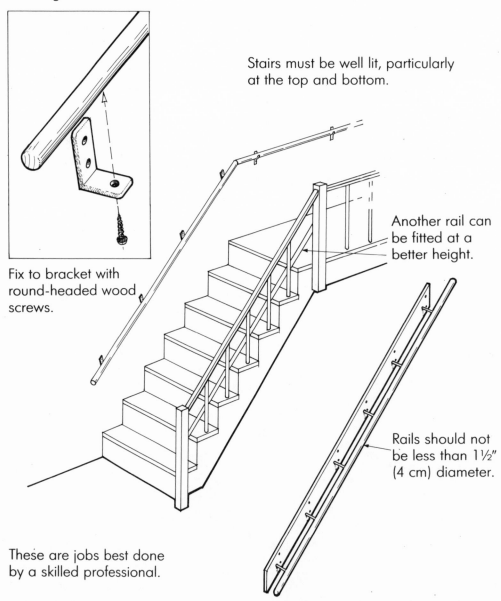

Stairs must be well lit, particularly at the top and bottom.

Another rail can be fitted at a better height.

Fix to bracket with round-headed wood screws.

Rails should not be less than 1½" (4 cm) diameter.

These are jobs best done by a skilled professional.

A complete assembly can be made ready to fix to the wall or bannister.

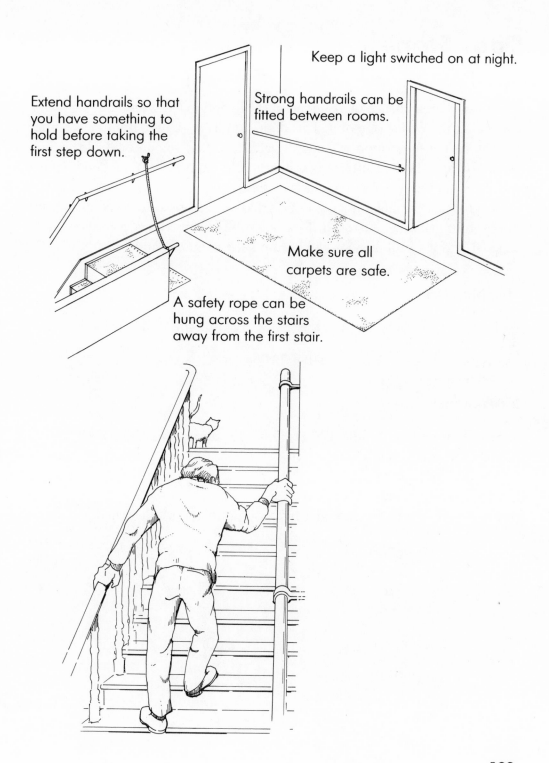

Extend handrails so that you have something to hold before taking the first step down.

Strong handrails can be fitted between rooms.

Keep a light switched on at night.

Make sure all carpets are safe.

A safety rope can be hung across the stairs away from the first stair.

Door Stops

There is always a chance of a sudden gust of wind making the door slam when you are on the wrong side of it. This door stop hangs by the front or back door and can be put in position without any effort, so that you are never locked out. Don't buy any special stuffing, as rolled up old clothes are quite good enough, and if it's not heavy enough add a few stones.

Doors inside the home may also be fitted with stops, and some of the ways these can be made are illustrated. To save having to bend down, a cord and hooks screwed into the wall or door will always keep them to hand.

Shopping List

A. Any piece of strong cloth at least 9″ × 12″ (23 cm × 30 cm)

B. String, length according to requirements

Instructions

1. Sew cloth to make a tube 4½″ (11.5 cm) diameter × 12″ (30 cm).
2. Stuff and sew up ends.
3. Sew on loops for string.
4. Attach string as illustrated.
5. Fix a hook beside the door and hang on door stop as illustrated.

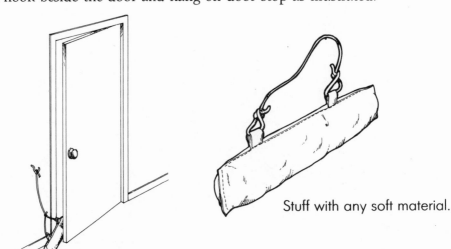

Stuff with any soft material.

Door stops should be brightly colored for visibility.

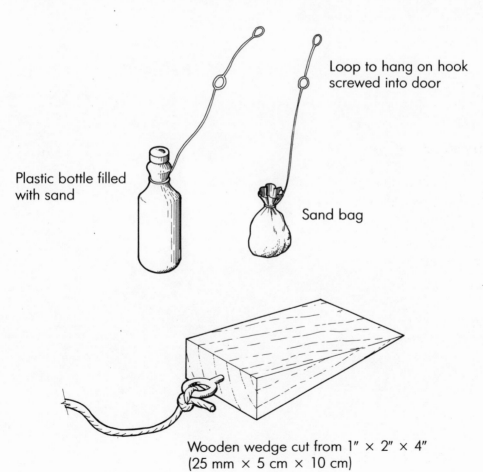

Loop to hang on hook screwed into door

Plastic bottle filled with sand

Sand bag

Wooden wedge cut from 1″ × 2″ × 4″ (25 mm × 5 cm × 10 cm)

GETTING FROM ROOM TO ROOM

When you have difficulty moving about, it is important to be well organized, so that you do not have to make a lot of unnecessary journeys to and fro to fetch articles you need. Bags can be fitted to any walking aid you may use to hold small, light objects, and well-stocked trolleys will provide both support and a handy way of transporting everything required for a particular job. The pocketed aprons and belts described in the KITCHEN and GARDEN sections will also be helpful.

Cleaning Cart

The cleaning cart is really a small wheeled walker with a shelf and tray. It will carry all the cleaning materials from room to room to save a lot of "to-ing and fro-ing" for forgotten things. If going up stairs is difficult, have a second cart up there and keep it in a closet out of sight when not in use. A few hooks around the tray side can be used to hang cleaning rags, dusters, and other things which have a string or tape loop. The shelf must not be too wide or you will bump your shins when walking, but there must be a shelf as it gives rigidity to the legs. If the cleaning cart has to be made higher or lower, don't forget to add in the height of the casters. If it has to be made wider or narrower, remember that all the other pieces will have a different length. Do not use this cart on a slippery floor, and be sure carpets are safe and will not catch in the wheels.

Shopping List

A. Back legs, 2 required: softwood 1½″ × 1½″ × 27″ (4 cm × 4 cm × 77.5 cm)

B. Front legs, 2 required: softwood 1½″ × 1½″ × 27″ (4 cm × 4 cm × 77.5 cm)

C. Sides, 4 required: softwood ½″ × 1½″ × 12″ (11 mm × 4 cm × 30 cm)

D. Shelf: plywood ¼″ × 6″ × 12″ (6 mm × 15 cm × 30 cm)

E. Shelf and tray fronts, 2 required: softwood ½″ × 1½″ × 12″ (11 mm × 4 cm × 30 cm)

F. Tray: plywood ¼″ × 12″ × 12″ (6 mm × 30 cm × 30 cm)

G. Cup hooks, 6-8 required

H. Casters, 4 required. The wheels should be about 2″ (5 cm) diameter.

Construction: Glue and Nail

Instructions

1. Cut a 45° angle to the top of legs A.
2. Fix sides C to legs A and B, the lower ones 12″ (30 cm) from the top.
3. Fix fronts E to legs B, the top one to the outside and the lower one to the inside.
4. Cut the corners of tray F to fit around the legs A and B.
5. Turn upside down and fit tray F and shelf D.
6. Fit casters.
7. Remove all sharp corners and edges, and sandpaper.
8. Paint or varnish.

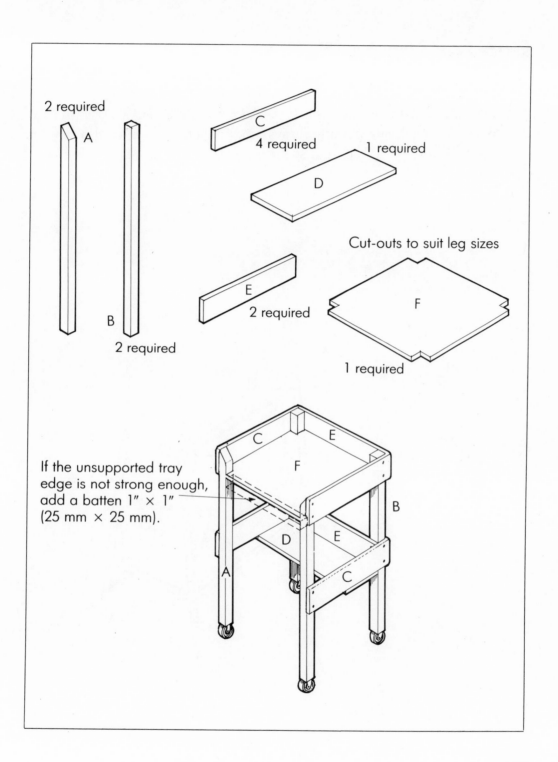

2 required

A

B

2 required

C

4 required

1 required

D

Cut-outs to suit leg sizes

E

2 required

F

1 required

C   E

F

If the unsupported tray
edge is not strong enough,
add a batten 1" × 1"
(25 mm × 25 mm).

B

D   E

A   C

Bag for Frame Walker

A suitable bag for a walker can easily be found in the stores and adapted to fit to the top rail. A string lacing is nearly always good enough, but it must also be fixed at the bottom to stop the bag from swinging.

This bag must only be used for small light things.

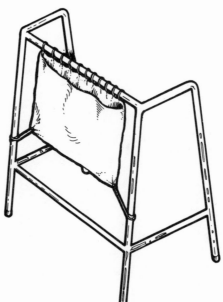

Walking Cane Bag

Like the crutch bag which follows, this must not be made too big and should only be used for small light articles. The metal clip may have to be made up by the local garage, but look into the hardware store first.

Shopping List

A. Bag support: plywood ¼″ × 1″ × 6″ (6 mm × 25 mm × 15 cm)

B. Metal clip. The size will depend on the diameter of the cane.

C. Nuts and bolts, 2 required: round-headed, about ½″ (12 mm) long

D. Bag cloth: 6″ wide × 12″ long (15 cm × 30 cm)

E. String for lacing

Instructions

1. Drill holes for metal clip nuts C.
2. Drill holes for string E.
3. Make bag D.
4. Lace bag D to bag support A.
5. Fix bag to cane with clip B and nuts and bolts C.

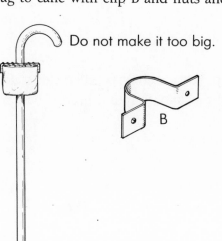

Do not make it too big.

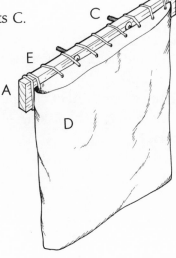

Crutch Bag

Most crutches can be fitted with this little bag which can hold a few personal things. If money or valuables are to be carried, it is advisable to fit a zipper or at least a button to help to protect them. Don't make the bag too big or put too much in it, as the extra weight might make it difficult to walk (and you may also upset your medical adviser).

The bag can either be laced or nailed to the front clamping piece.

Shopping List

A. Clamping strips, 2 required: softwood ½″ × 1½″ (11 mm × 4 cm) × the outside width of the crutch plus 2″ (5 cm)

B. Nuts and bolts, 2 of each required. The length will be the thickness of the crutch plus 1″ plus ½″ (25 mm plus 12 mm). Try and buy roofing nuts and bolts, as these have a round head which will not catch on your clothing.

C. Cloth to make a small bag about 7″ wide × 16″ long (18 cm × 40 cm)

D. Round-headed upholstery nails, about 10

E. (Optional: self-sticking cloth fastening)

Instructions

1. Drill the holes for the nuts and bolts B through clamping strips A.
2. Sew up bag C.
3. Nail or lace to front clamping strip. (Or attach with self-sticking cloth.)
4. Clamp to crutch, making sure that the smooth round-headed bolt head is on the body.

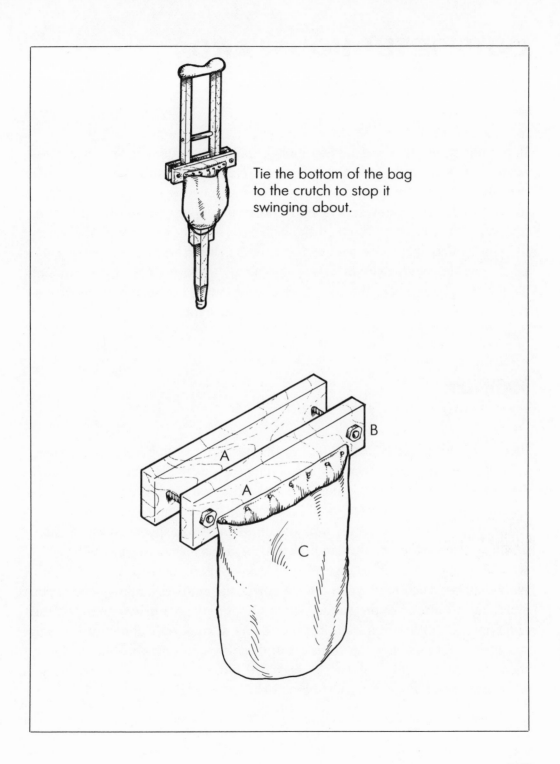

Tie the bottom of the bag to the crutch to stop it swinging about.

A

B

A

C

OUTSIDE THE HOUSE AND IN THE GARDEN

If you find yourself becoming less mobile, there are many simple but effective adaptations you can make which will allow you to go out and about as much as you like. A ramp will overcome difficulties in negotiating steps, a little shelf for deliveries will mean you will not have to worry about bending down to pick them up, and a letter box will catch all the mail before it lands on the floor.

In the garden, there is no limit to the changes that can be made to enable you to enjoy tending your plants. Bring the flowerbeds up to your level, fix handrails along paths, make use of hanging baskets and tables. Gardening is one activity that is infinitely adaptable and should never be beyond your reach, no matter how disabled you may be.

Ramps

Ramps should always be made and fixed in position by a local contractor unless there is a member of the family who has the necessary skills. This is one of those jobs which looks easy but is not, and any fixing which has to be done to the building can prove expensive should the wall or step be damaged. If the ramp is not securely fixed at both ends, gaps and unevenness will appear sooner or later.

The angle or slope of the ramp should be as shallow as space will permit, whether it is to be used by a wheelchair or for walking up and down. Carefully work out how much room you have, and make the ramp as gentle a slope as possible. The treatment of the surface is very important. No matter what weather conditions are likely to prevail, it must be safe to walk on. Sand scattered onto wet paint can give a non-slip surface, but it soon wears smooth. Whatever treatment is given it must be regularly inspected. A builder can make a permanent job using cement, and make the surface non-slip before it sets.

Keep the gradient at not less than 1:12.

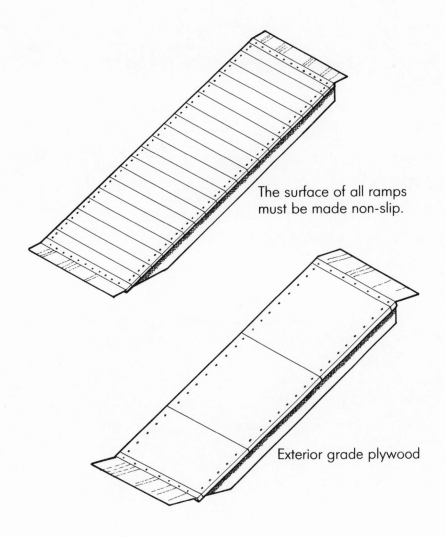

The surface of all ramps must be made non-slip.

Exterior grade plywood

Delivery Shelf

A shelf by the front or back door can save a lot of bending down, because all deliveries can be left on it. A stiff length of thick wire or strip of metal can be bent as illustrated to stop light packages from blowing away.

Shopping List

A. Shelf: softwood ¾″ × 6″ × 12″ (19 mm × 15 cm × 30 cm)

B. Brackets, 2 required: strong, well-painted shelf brackets to take a 12″ (30 cm) wide shelf

C. Rail: stiff, thick wire or metal strip ³⁄₃₂″ × ½″ × 27″ (2 mm × 12 mm × 67.5 cm)

D. Clothes peg to hold notes

Instructions

1. Fix brackets B to shelf A.
2. Mark wall for screws.
3. Paint shelf A.
4. For masonry walls, drill and plug wall for screws.
5. Fix shelf to wall and check that it is strong enough.
6. Bend the wire to shape or drill and bend the metal strip and shape as illustrated to make the rail.
7. Paint the rail.
8. Fix the clothes peg as illustrated.

You don't have to bend
down to pick up the milk
and other deliveries.
Have a shelf made.

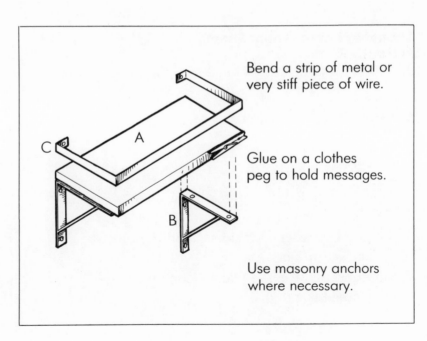

Bend a strip of metal or
very stiff piece of wire.

Glue on a clothes
peg to hold messages.

Use masonry anchors
where necessary.

Letter Box

Where there is a mail slot in the door, another aid to save bending down is a box to catch letters and newspapers. If there is no room for a box because the door opens against a wall, an illustration shows how to make a box from soft foam which will flatten when it touches the wall.

Shopping List (All pieces cut from one plank.)

A. Sides, 2 required: softwood ½″ × 6″ × 12″ (11 mm × 15 cm × 30 cm)

B. Front: softwood ½″ × 12″ × 12″ (11 mm × 30 cm × 30 cm)

C. Base: softwood ½″ × 6″ × 13″ (11 mm × 15 cm × 32.5 cm)

D. Brackets, 4 required: see illustration

Shopping List for Foam Sheet

A. Fairly stiff foam sheet about 1″ (25 mm) thick, all other sizes as above

Construction: Glue and Nail

Instructions

1. To make front B, glue 2 pieces of wood together.
2. Fix sides A to front B.
3. Fix base C to assembled sides A and front B.
4. Fix brackets to sides A.
5. Sandpaper and paint to match door.
6. Fix finished box to door.

Letters don't have to drop on the mat. Have a box fitted.

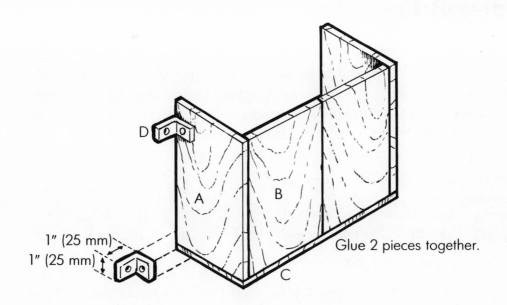

D

1" (25 mm)
1" (25 mm)

A   B

C

Glue 2 pieces together.

Don't put screws into the
end grain of base C.

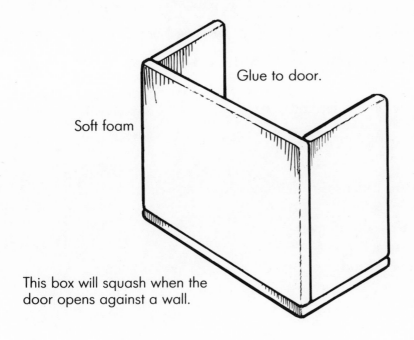

Glue to door.

Soft foam

This box will squash when the
door opens against a wall.

Garden Kneeler

As you grow older the ground seems to be further away. A kneeler that enables you to get down to the low gardening jobs, as well as helping you up to a standing position again, may make it possible for you to continue gardening for a long time to come. It is important to get the measurement for the kneeler right, and it may be necessary to change the height of the sides for you.

Shopping List

A. Sides, 2 required: softwood ¾" × 8" × 16" (19 mm × 20 cm × 40 cm)

B. Kneeling board: softwood ¾" × 8" × 14" (19 mm × 20 cm × 35 cm)

C. Kneeling board battens, 2 required: softwood 1" × 1" × 8" (25 mm × 25 mm × 20 cm)

D. Base: softwood ¾" × 8" × 14" (19 mm × 20 cm × 35 cm)

E. Base battens, 2 required: softwood 1" × 1" × 8" (25 mm × 25 mm × 20 cm)

F. Support: softwood ¾" (19 mm) × to suit kneeling height × 14" (35 cm)

G. Support battens, 2 required: 1" × 1" × 10" (25 mm × 25 mm × 25 cm)

Construction: Waterproof Glue and Screw

Instructions

1. Fix kneeling board battens C to sides A at kneeling height.
2. Fix battens E to base D.
3. Fix support battens G to support F.
4. Fix sides A to assembled base D.
5. Fix support F to center of base D.

6. Fix kneeling board B to sides A and support F.
7. Sandpaper and paint.
8. Pad top edges of sides A.
9. Pad kneeling board.

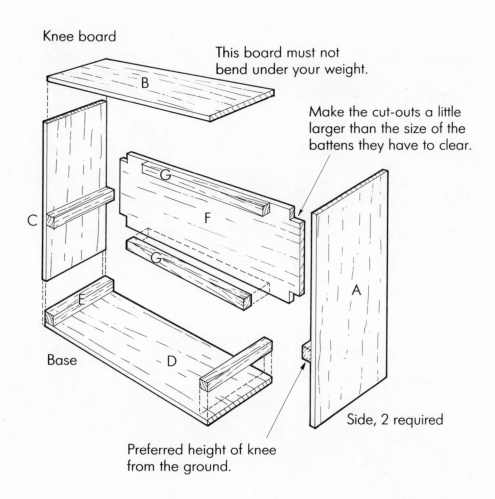

Knee board

This board must not
bend under your weight.

Make the cut-outs a little
larger than the size of the
battens they have to clear.

B

C

G

F

G

E

A

Base

D

Side, 2 required

Preferred height of knee
from the ground.

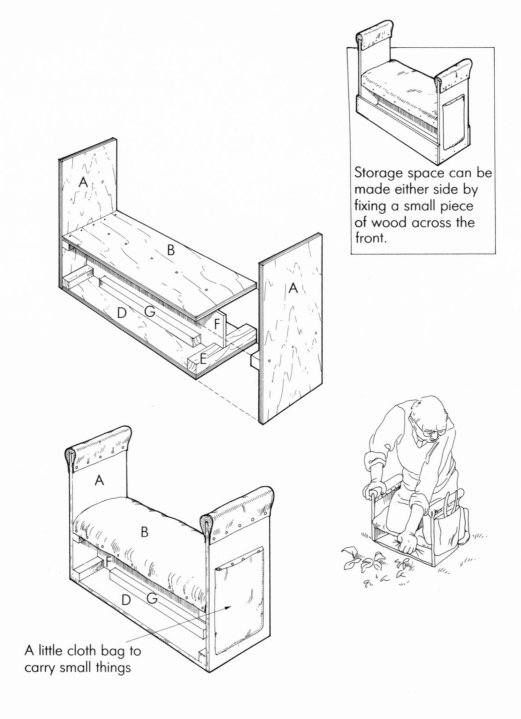

Storage space can be made either side by fixing a small piece of wood across the front.

A little cloth bag to carry small things

158

Boot and Shoe Cleaner

It's not a good idea to go into the house with dirty boots and leave the floor covered with muddy foot marks. Keep these cleaners hanging somewhere handy for use on those days when the soil is sticky.

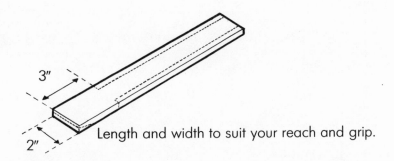

3"

2"

Length and width to suit your reach and grip.

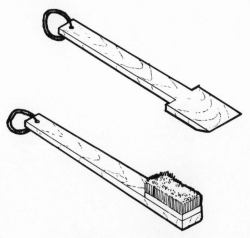

Wooden backed brush. Attach with screws.

Gardening Seat and Tool Box

There are lots of gardening jobs which can be done while sitting down on a low, comfortable seat. This seat also holds a few tools, which can save you going backwards and forwards to the shed to fetch the ones that have been forgotten. A rope is tied to one end so that it can be pulled along.

Shopping List

A. Top: softwood ¾″ × 8¾″ × 13½″ (19 mm × 22 cm × 34 cm)

B. Sides, 2 required: softwood ¾″ × 8″ × 8″ (19 mm × 20 cm × 20 cm)

C. Back: softwood ¾″ × 8″ × 13½″ (19 mm × 20 cm × 34 cm)

D. Base: softwood ¾″ × 8″ × 12″ (19 mm × 20 cm × 30 cm)

E. Front: softwood ¾″ × 2¾″ × 13½″ (19 mm × 7 cm × 34 cm)

F. Soft rope: length to suit your height

Construction: Glue and Screw

Instructions

1. Drill 2 holes for rope in side B.
2. Fix sides B to base D.
3. Fix back C to assembled base D.
4. Fix front E to assembled base D.
5. Fix top A to sides B and back C.
6. Sandpaper and paint.
7. Pad top A. The padding should be covered with strong cloth.

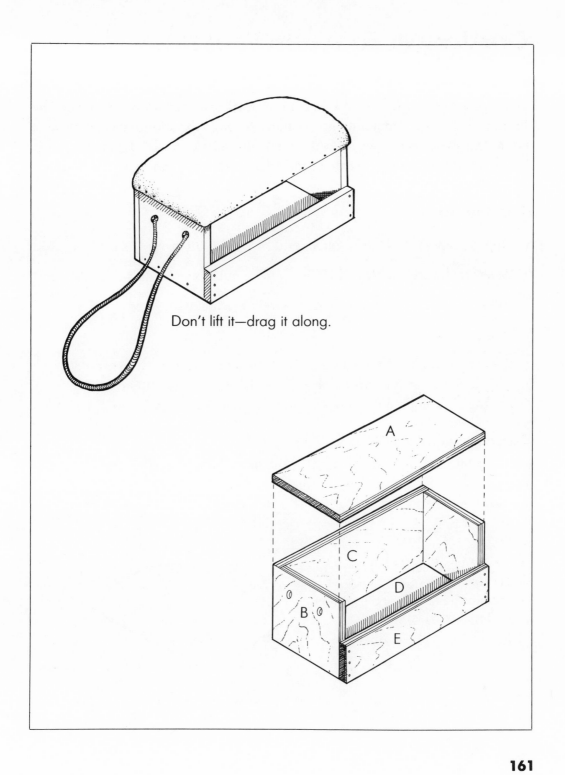

Don't lift it—drag it along.

Kneeling Pad

Kneeling can be tough on the knees, but a thick pad can be a great help. The choice of padding is important because if the knees go too far into it you will soon start to feel all the stones again. As the grass and soil are usually damp, it's a good idea to make one side of waterproof material, so that the padding will keep dry.

Shopping List

A. Strong cloth such as canvas: about 12″ × 18″ (30 cm × 46 cm)

B. Waterproof cloth such as oil cloth, vinyl: about 9″ × 12″ (23 cm × 30 cm)

C. Padding (Foam, cotton padding, or layered remnants.)

Instructions

1. Fold cloth A in half to make a bag 9″ × 12″ (23 cm × 30 cm).
2. Sew together along one short side and the long side to make an open-ended bag.
3. Sew waterproof cloth on to one side.
4. Evenly fill the bag, making sure that the filling is firm, and sew up remaining sides.
5. Sew on handle.

A polyethylene bag can be used as an inner waterproof bag, but it must have some holes on the top side to let the air out.

Use a waterproof material for the bottom.

Handrails

Always buy wood which you find good to touch and hold. It need not necessarily be round or "D" shaped, but it must be smooth and completely free of splits, twists, and splinters. The posts must be pointed at one end and long enough to be driven or dug well into the ground. (The wood must be treated against rot.) The complete structure must be strong enough to take your weight should you stumble.

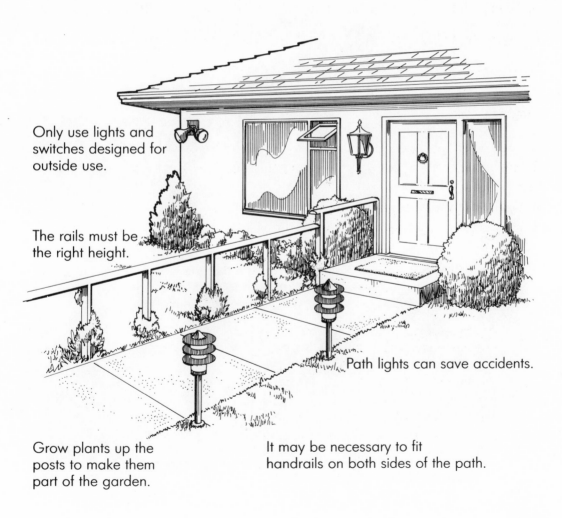

Only use lights and switches designed for outside use.

The rails must be the right height.

Path lights can save accidents.

Grow plants up the posts to make them part of the garden.

It may be necessary to fit handrails on both sides of the path.

Garden Adaptations

If you have a garden area, there is nothing to stop you making aids or having a few made, and planning a few changes to the garden layout, which will enable you to go on getting pleasure from growing things. Much of the heavy work may have to be left to others, but a few ideas are given on the following pages which may help you to go on enjoying this wonderful pastime for a long time.

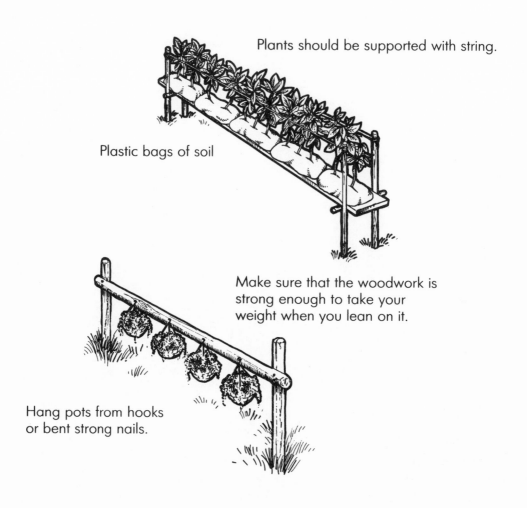

Plants should be supported with string.

Plastic bags of soil

Make sure that the woodwork is strong enough to take your weight when you lean on it.

Hang pots from hooks or bent strong nails.

Let the plants have plenty of light.

Make small drain holes.

Wire hanging baskets can be
used. To stop them swinging
in the wind, tie to the ground.

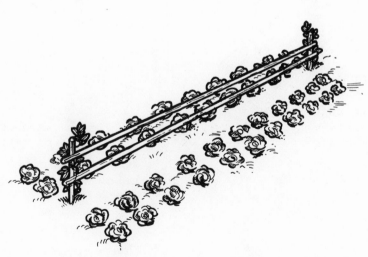

The lower rail helps you when bending down to tend the plants.

A net between 2 posts for climbing plants.

All posts must be driven well into the ground.

A shelf can be used for seed boxes.

MINI GREENHOUSE

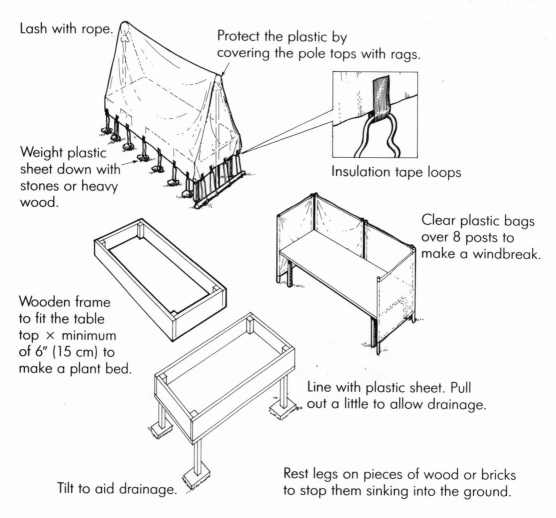

Lash with rope.

Protect the plastic by covering the pole tops with rags.

Weight plastic sheet down with stones or heavy wood.

Insulation tape loops

Clear plastic bags over 8 posts to make a windbreak.

Wooden frame to fit the table top × minimum of 6″ (15 cm) to make a plant bed.

Line with plastic sheet. Pull out a little to allow drainage.

Tilt to aid drainage.

Rest legs on pieces of wood or bricks to stop them sinking into the ground.

A plastic sheet helps
to keep the table clean.

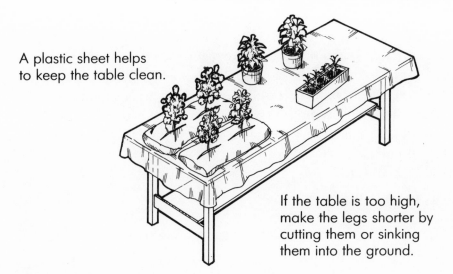

If the table is too high,
make the legs shorter by
cutting them or sinking
them into the ground.

Pad the tops of the
posts and tie a strong
string between them.

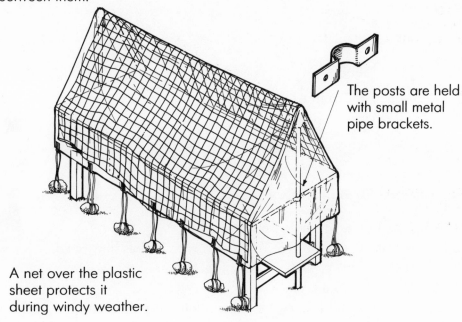

The posts are held
with small metal
pipe brackets.

A net over the plastic
sheet protects it
during windy weather.

Four-Wheeled Box Trolley

A little trolley to carry tools and things can save many trips back to the toolshed, and it can also be used to bring in the harvest. Details are given on how to make a box, but any reasonably strong crate can be used. The wheels should be large, with a wide tread, but if the ground is very rough it may be better to fit skids, as illustrated. It is not always necessary to make a trolley with front-wheel steering, but it does help if pulling is a problem.

Shopping List for Box Trolley

A. Axle, 2 required: ½" (12 mm) diameter metal tube or steel rod, or threaded redirod, to suit wheels and width of box

B. Brackets, 4 required: pipe brackets, or bend a piece of stiff metal

C. Box bottom, 2 pieces required: softwood ¾" × 6" × 18" (19 mm × 15 cm × 45 cm)

D. Box sides, 2 required: softwood ¾" × 6" × 18" (19 mm × 15 cm × 45 cm)

E. Box ends, 2 required: softwood ¾" × 6" × 10½" (19 mm × 15 cm × 26.5 cm)

F. Skids when wheels are not used, 2 required: softwood ¾" × 6" × 18" (19 mm × 15 cm × 45 cm)

G. Wheels, 4 required: any with wide tread, minimum diameter 4" (10 cm)

Instructions for Box Trolley

1. Assemble box as illustrated on page 171.
2. Fix brackets B about 3" (7.5 cm) from each end as illustrated.
3. Drill a small hole at each end of axles A to hold fixing wire.
4. Slide axles A through brackets B.
5. Fix on wheels and insert wire in axle holes to hold them in place.
6. Drill holes for tow rope.

Shopping List for Steered Trolley

A. Axle, 2 required: metal tube or steel rod to suit wheels, width of box, and board

B. Axle brackets, 4 wanted: diameter to suit axles

C. Box bottom, 2 pieces required: softwood ¾″ × 6″ × 18″ (19 mm × 15 cm × 45 cm)

D. Box sides, 2 required: softwood ¾″ × 6″ × 18″ (19 mm × 15 cm × 45 cm)

E. Box ends, 2 required: softwood ¾″ × 6″ × 10½″ (19 mm × 15 cm × 26.5 cm)

F. Board: softwood about ¾″ × 10″ × 32″ (19 mm × 25 cm × 80 cm)

G. Axle board: softwood ¾″ (19 mm) × 3″ (7.5 cm) × width of box plus 2″ (5 cm)

H. Bolt, 2 washers, and 2 nuts: bolt length to suit total thickness of wood plus washers and nuts

I. Wheels, 4 required: as for box trolley

Instructions for Steered Trolley

1. Drill board F to be a good fit for bolt H.
2. Drill axle board G for bolt H and tow ropes.
3. Fix brackets B to axle board G.
4. Fix brackets B to back of box.
5. Fix board F so that it does not get in the way of axle—allow 3½″ (9 cm).
6. Fix axles and wheels as for box trolley.
7. Bolt axle board G to board F so that it can move easily.
8. Tie on tow rope.

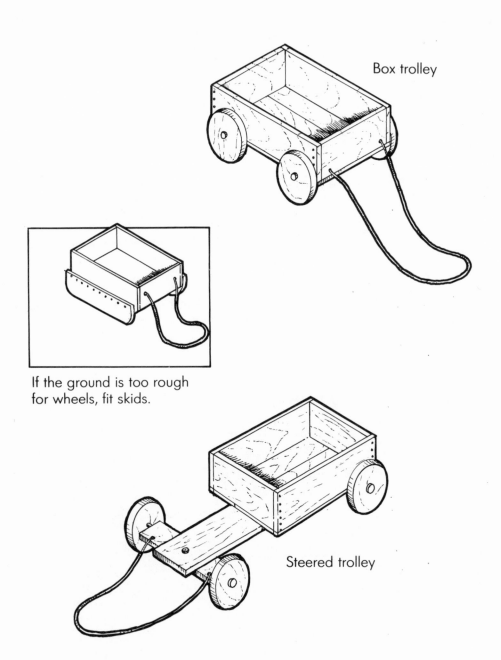

Box trolley

If the ground is too rough
for wheels, fit skids.

Steered trolley

BOX TROLLEY

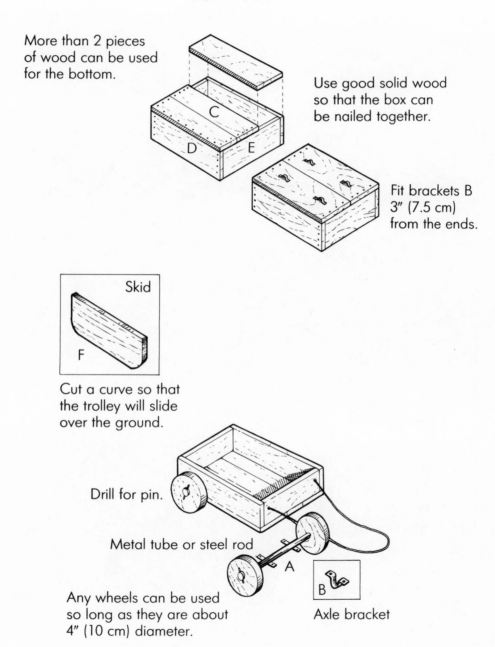

More than 2 pieces
of wood can be used
for the bottom.

Use good solid wood
so that the box can
be nailed together.

C

D   E

Fit brackets B
3″ (7.5 cm)
from the ends.

Skid

F

Cut a curve so that
the trolley will slide
over the ground.

Drill for pin.

Metal tube or steel rod

A

Any wheels can be used
so long as they are about
4″ (10 cm) diameter.

B

Axle bracket

STEERED TROLLEY

Leave 3½" (9 cm).

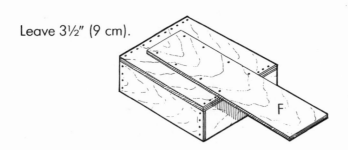

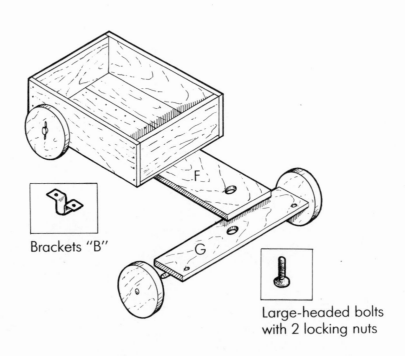

Brackets "B"

Large-headed bolts
with 2 locking nuts

Two-Wheeled Trolley

A two-wheeled trolley is sometimes easier to manouver than a four-wheeled one. As all the weight is to be borne on two wheels it is advisable to use large, wide ones which will not sink into the soft soil so much. Wooden boxes can sometimes be obtained from produce stores.

Shopping List

A. Towing arm: softwood ½″ × 3″ × 36″ (11 mm × 7.5 cm × 90 cm)

B. Handle: softwood 1″ × 1½″ × 9″ (25 mm × 4 cm × 22.5 cm)

C. Stop: softwood 1″ × 3″ × 3″ (25 mm × 7.5 cm × 7.5 cm)

D. Brackets, 2 required: to suit axle
   Refer to Four-Wheeled Trolley for details of box.

Instructions

1. Fix handle B to towing arm A.
2. Fix stop C to towing arm A.
3. Fix assembled towing arm down center line of box bottom. See illustration for other information.
4. Fix wheel axle to box with brackets D. (See illustrations.)

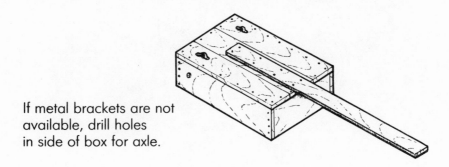

If metal brackets are not available, drill holes in side of box for axle.

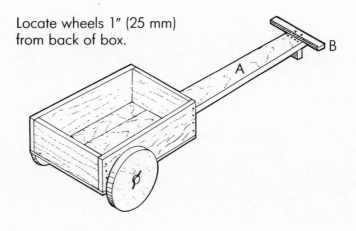

Locate wheels 1″ (25 mm) from back of box.

B

A

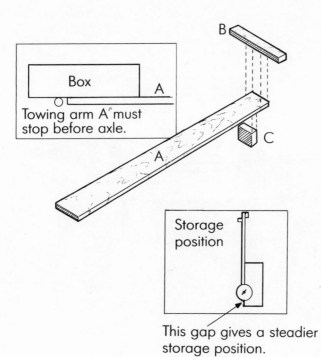

Box

A

Towing arm A must stop before axle.

B

A

C

Storage position

This gap gives a steadier storage position.

Canvas Belt with Pockets

This simple belt with pockets can be used in the garden as well as around the house when doing odd jobs. It is also a very useful belt to wear for some hobbies.

Shopping List

A. A length of canvas or strong cloth about 8″ × 20″ (20 cm × 50 cm)

Instructions

1. Hem both long sides of canvas.
2. Fold canvas in half lengthwise and sew pockets.
3. Sew on 2 loops of canvas as illustrated for tapes or string.
4. (Optional: Make tape extra long to allow tying in front. Or finish with self-stick cloth for closing.)

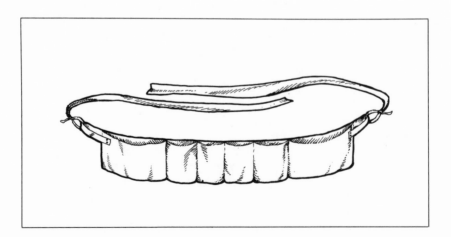

Cloth Belt with Pockets and Hooks

Sometimes a belt on which can hang clippers, scissors, or a knife, plus a few little pockets to put odds and ends in, is all that is needed when puttering around the garden.

Shopping List

A. Length of canvas or strong cloth about 20″ (50 cm) long × 3″ (7.5 cm) wide

B. Length of cloth for bags about 8″ × 12″ (20 cm × 30 cm). This will make 4 bags of 3″ × 4″ (7.5 cm × 10 cm).

C. Hooks bought or made from stiff wire and shaped as illustrated

Instructions

1. Fold cloth B and sew to make 4 bags.
2. Shape and hem canvas A to make belt.
3. Sew bags to canvas belt A.
4. Bend wire to make hooks C.
5. Sew hooks C to canvas belt A.
6. Sew tapes or string to canvas belt A.

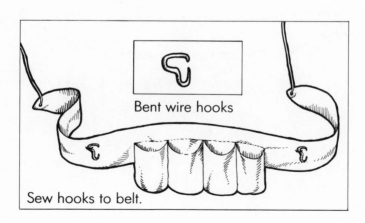

Bent wire hooks

Sew hooks to belt.

APPENDIX
From the publisher, Hartley & Marks.

Standard Handrails

Because bathroom safety is of particular concern, and because it is not easy to make and correctly install safe and reliable bathroom aids, here are some examples of grab bars and safety rails available from medical supply companies. (Ordinary plumbing and bathroom shops do not supply these, and standard towel bars are too weak to give safe support.) Your medical adviser should be consulted for help in selecting and installing suitable grab bars or tub rails.

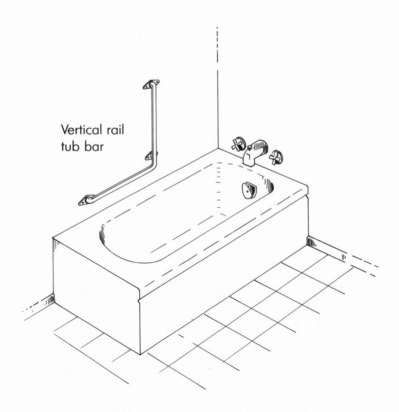

Vertical rail
tub bar

TUB RAILS

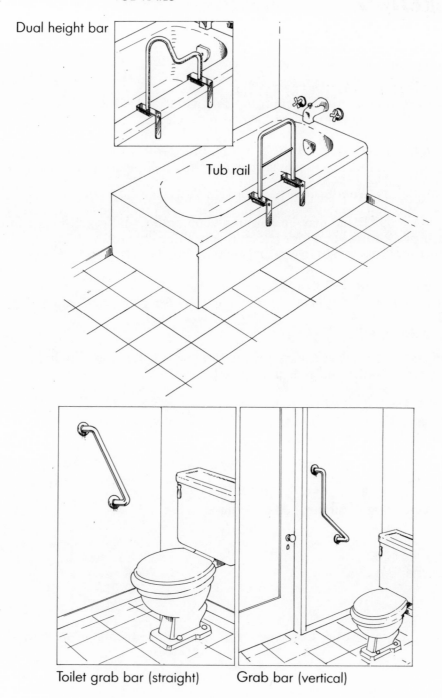

Dual height bar

Tub rail

Toilet grab bar (straight)

Grab bar (vertical)

179